HOW TO MANAGE YOUR
MONEY

BY JOHN KIRK

A BENJAMIN COMPANY BOOK
NEW YORK

SBN 87502–007–0

Library of Congress Catalog Card Number LC 66-26201

Copyright © 1966, by

Specialized Publishing Company

All rights reserved

Published by

The Benjamin Company, Inc.

485 Madison Avenue, New York, N.Y.

Printed in the United States of America

Ninth Printing: March 1974

Foreword

You may well be opening this book at a critically important moment in your financial life.

Whether you are a teen-ager or are celebrating your twenty-fifth wedding anniversary, a housewife or a successful businessman, a factory worker, clerk, secretary, salesman, farmer, professional man or are retired—you will find here hundreds of money- and time-saving tips.

Do you need a mortgage to help you purchase a home, or a loan to help you furnish it? Are you planning to go on a honeymoon or buy a car? Are you wondering how to find the right bank for your new savings and checking accounts? In this book, you'll find the practical answers to these everyday financial questions.

Are you considering investing extra dollars in stocks? Or seeking a sound savings plan for your children's college education? Or thinking about establishing a trust or setting up an estate? In this clearly written book, you will get valuable information and the no-nonsense guidance you want.

Of course, you know how vitally significant money management is to your financial peace of mind today and your hopes for your family's way of life tomorrow; you wouldn't be opening this book in the first place if you weren't aware of how much is at stake. Yet, many people—particularly young people, starting a career, or beginning marriage and a family of their own—shrug off the extent to which they themselves can use money management to enrich their lives over the years.

"Oh well, when we get old and have lots of money," they say, "we'll worry about managing the money. Right now, with our income, it's all we can do just to pay the bills each month."

But that's precisely the point! It is even more crucial for young people to manage their money properly, in the early stages of their money-earning lifetime, than it is for the more established, older family with a greater income and nest egg. (The older couple wouldn't have the income and nest egg, if they hadn't learned how to manage when they were young.) It is when every dollar counts that careful handling of savings, insurance and loans is most important. It is when the family is starting out that it should develop healthy money-management habits, set up a system of monthly planning of income versus expenses and decide on long-term financial goals.

Much of the material published on money management is defiantly technical and dull; you, the reader, have to fight your way through it, and you often end up detesting the whole subject. This book, however, is written in such a straightforward, simple style that the basics—ranging from monthly budgeting to interest rate calculations—can be easily grasped by anyone. The thirty-two page workbook in the center is also an innovation which will provide you with a convenient way to keep track of every facet of your financial affairs.

In short, by following the sound advice in these pages and by using the book's effective aids, you should be able to save thousands of dollars—and hundreds of headaches.

An important feature is the book's thorough—and thoroughly understandable—explanation of the many facilities offered by your full-service commercial bank. It will give you a new appreciation of the major role your bank—and your full-service banker—plays in your life.

Successful money management and successful living go hand in hand in our society. They are actually inseparable. They complement each other and they add to each other. You will find this a valuable, consistently useful guide to achieving both—no matter who you are or what your income level, age, occupation, or family responsibilities.

Sylvia F. Porter

Contents

Introduction

Suppose you were given a flourishing money tree, and suppose, too, that you had a green thumb and knew what was needed to produce a harvest of crisp green bills. The solution to all your problems? Not at all. Chances are you would find yourself as financially strained as ever—because you wouldn't know the best ways to handle your fine new crop of dollars.

The ability to use money efficiently is not a natural act. It has to be learned, just as we have to learn to read and write. Unlike reading and writing, however, the ABC's of managing money are not ordinarily taught in school. That's why most people don't really know how to use what money they do have wisely. They've never learned the basic principles. They juggle their finances like an untrained seal with a ball that is forever dropping and rolling away without purpose—just as most dollars seem to do.

If you sometimes feel that you are not really in command of your money, if you cannot make your dollars go as far as they might, you are not alone. After all, it's no small task to meet monthly payments, to find funds for needed clothing and appliances, to set up a budget and keep checking accounts balanced, and to have enough money left over for many other needs and desires.

The rules of money management apply equally for male and female. If only the husband works, the wife should be as informed as the wage earner about what happens to their dollars. Single working girls, widows, unmarried men—all face common money problems. That is why the fundamentals in this handbook can apply to anyone who has income. The purpose of this book is to provide you, the reader, with money know-how, to show you the ABC's of financial management.

In the pages that follow, you will find new ideas and useful suggestions designed to stretch your pay check, and to create for you more enjoyment from your money, while sweeping away confusion and frustration. The new knowledge gained will help toward your financial stability, making for smoother family life and brightening your point of view in general. Should you feel that you are already doing a fairly good job of money management and are indeed making ends meet, you may find that with a study of the fresh facts presented here, your "stretch" will have even greater elasticity.

Whatever your financial concern—auto loan, mortgage, budget, or investment—you can quickly turn to this handbook for practical and easy-to-understand guidance.

All of us should improve our money-management techniques. After all, if you are the male breadwinner in your family, you will earn $200,000 to $300,000 (or more) in your lifetime. And that, certainly, is a large enough sum to warrant the best possible care.

CHAPTER ONE

How Much Money Do You Really Have?

The first step toward effective money management is getting an accurate figure on exactly how much money you have to manage each year.

Doesn't everyone know how much his family has to manage every year? Surprisingly, the answer is usually, no. All of us tend, for the most part, either to overestimate or underestimate. Let's take a closer look at the problem. Asked how much your family has to manage each year, the odds are you will promptly answer "$6,590," or whatever the annual income of the wage earner is.

If you answer this way, you're wrong! Here's why: When you answer the question by giving the gross figure, or the annual salary, that is not what you need to know. You need to know the *net* figure—the amount of money left after Federal withholding taxes, after hospitalization premium deductions, after social security payments, after savings bond deductions, after state withholding taxes, and, in some cases, after union dues deductions.

You can see that it's easy to overestimate how much money is under your management control. Now, let's look at the other 11 side of the coin. Once again, "How much do you have to manage each year?" This time, instead of giving the gross figure of $6,590, you multiply the take-home pay from one pay check by the number of pay checks received each year. Then your answer becomes "$5,100."

And once again we say you're wrong.

Why? Because now you underestimated the amount of money you have under your control. You forgot to include a Christmas bonus. You overlooked the fact that your teen-age daughter contributed half of her summer earnings to the family. You didn't remember the interest from your savings account. In fact, there are many, many sources from which you may be getting additional income.

Here are other examples:

- *Money from the sale of a house, a car or a litter of pedigreed puppies*
- *Repayment of money lent by you*
- *Inheritances*
- *Gifts of cash on Christmas, birthdays, wedding anniversaries*
- *Winnings from gambling*
- *Payments from a life or casualty insurance policy*
- *Sales commissions*
- *Rents from tenants*
- *Tax refunds—both state and Federal*
- *Alimony payments*
- *Benefits from retirement or pension plans*
- *Payments from profit-sharing plans*
- *Interest from bonds*
- *Dividends and money from the sale of stocks*

No doubt there are other sources in your particular case. In the 32-page workbook section that follows Page 64, you will find a personal worksheet and permanent money record to help **12** you analyze your own income picture.

How sound is your sense of financial reality?

Why is it important to know exactly how many dollars you have to manage each year? Think of it this way: When you invite friends over to dinner, you count heads in advance to be sure that you are properly prepared—enough to eat, enough places set at the table and enough chairs to go around. Now, suppose a guest phones at the last 'minute and asks if he can bring extra visitors. You quickly assess how far you can stretch your planned provisions, and, knowing what extras can be added from the shelves, you reply that it is quite all right, or you say regretfully that it can't be managed.

For much the same reasons, it's wise to know ahead of time what the contents of the family treasury are. Can you anticipate having enough on hand to meet the unforeseen, the extra money you need for unanticipated expenses?

Without this inventory of real worth, you may lose touch with financial reality. This generally happens when income is overestimated. The head of the house who earns $10,000 a year in gross salary, for example, may quite easily—and falsely —feel financially self-satisfied. Yet, the worker with four children who grosses $10,000 has roughly $8,700 in take-home pay—assuming Federal tax withholding, state tax withholding, and social security deductions. The family obviously must not count on spending a nonexistent $1,300 of income that didn't come home.

You may waste precious dollars. This is bound to happen if you overlook some very real sources of income. That extra money won't actually be lost, but, if it is unexpected and unplanned for, it won't be put to its best advantage. Those dollars will become "extra" money and will be unaccountably frittered away, while your hard-earned salary dollars will be forced to work overtime in your behalf.

It makes sound financial sense, then, to figure out as accurately as possible what your total net yearly income is. Some extra sources of income are unpredictable, of course.

Just as a corporation prepares a balance sheet, your family **13** should set down on paper at regular intervals its assets and liabilities. That way—by learning how much you own and how much you owe—you'll be able to chart your financial progress.

How to figure your net worth

When your assets, or what you own, outweigh your liabilities, or what you owe, the dollar difference is called your "net worth." When liabilities are greater than assets, the difference is called "net loss." Of course, you should strive to have a net worth, not a net loss.

Let's work jointly on a sample balance sheet. Once you have had some practice, you can make out your own family's personal balance sheet.

We begin by adding up all you own—your assets. There are five asset categories:

Actual dollars. You have $85 in cash, another $185 in the checking account and $312 in a joint savings account. Total cash: $582.

Investments. You own ten shares of a common stock worth $255. You also have $1,000 invested in mutual fund shares. Total investments: $1,255.

Cash surrender value of permanent life insurance policies. You can quickly determine the cash value of your life policies by consulting the cash-surrender-value table in each policy. (The value of each policy gets higher as the policy grows older.) Let's say your policies this year are worth a total of $710.

Real estate. You own the house in which you live. It's worth $18,300. We'll talk about the mortgage later. Under assets, put the full market value of the house—whether you paid that much for it or not.

Market value of personal belongings. Include your furniture, appliances, TV sets, clothing, automobile, books, garden tools, etc. (Understand that market value of such secondhand items is low. Be conservative in your estimate.) In this sample, let's say, if you were forced to sell such personal belongings, you **14** could raise $850. (See center section, Page **3w.**, for a personal, permanent record page to figure the estimated worth of all of your valuables.)

Now add up these five categories to find the total of your present assets: $21,697.

Against total assets we place total liabilities. To begin, calculate how much more must be paid on your mortgage. Call this amount "Mortgage Payable." You have yet to pay: $13,000.

Now add up all the money you owe on installment loans— loans for the car, the new freezer, the TV set, the power mower. This is the installment loan category. You owe: $450.

Write down underneath the title "Accounts Payable," all the money you owe on a charge account basis. Include the drugstore, milkman, light company, telephone company, department stores and any others. You owe: $155.

Now total up all other bills outstanding—everything from the 35 cents you owe the newspaper delivery boy to a $500 dental bill. Write your total—in your case it's $600—under the heading "Unpaid Bills."

Finally, determine your unpaid real estate taxes—if any. Put that amount down under the heading "Unpaid Taxes." On such taxes you owe: $45.

Once you add those five liability categories, you'll discover that you have $14,250 in liabilities.

Your net worth—$21,697 in assets, less $14,250 in liabilities—is $7,447.

Hold on, now. Don't think for a moment you can put your hands on that $7,447. You can't—obviously. But that net-worth total, when computed each year, will give you a good running yardstick to help you determine how well you and your family are progressing financially.

If your net worth continues to increase, you are doing well. If it declines or simply holds steady, you had better take heed and find out what's wrong.

Now that we understand real income and net worth, we must consider expenses and habits of spending. **15**

CHAPTER TWO

The Financial Necessities

Stereo, hi-fi sets and expensive sports cars are nice to have. So are vacations in Europe, dinners in good restaurants and tickets to Broadway plays.

Notice the key word "nice." The word implies that such things aren't absolutely necessary. But since we all deserve at least a few of the nice things in life, isn't there something we can do about it? Definitely! That is the purpose of this chapter— to help you put your financial house in order, so that you can safely enjoy some of the nice things the world has to offer.

Comparing your family's spending to the average

Recently the National Industrial Conference Board issued a report based on statistics compiled by the Bureau of Labor. Let's examine these figures as an interesting and important guide for your own discussions.

The report found that food consumes only about 24 per cent of the average American family's expenditures. Rent, mortgage payments, insurance on the home, property taxes, home maintenance and improvement now also account for 24 per cent of the average family's budget. Household furnishings, appliances and equipment take another 5 per cent. Ten per cent is the figure for shoes and clothing. About 9½ per cent on the average is spent on medical insurance, doctor bills, drugs and medicine, plus personal care items such as haircuts, cosmetics and the beauty parlor. Transportation—the family car, automobile insurance, commuting to work, long-distance travel—takes 15 per cent. Three and a half per cent is spent on tobacco and alcohol, 4 per cent on recreation, about 2 per cent on reading and education, and approximately 2 per cent on all other expenditures, including gifts, life insurance, contributions, allowances and interest on loans.

On Page 25 of this chapter is a chart which represents a more detailed account of these statistics. They certainly make interesting reading, but it's important for us to remember that the percentages may vary from family to family, and that certain expenditures—travel, liquor, clothing—do fluctuate widely from low- to high-income groups. For our purposes, therefore, we will use this report simply as a rough model for comparison with your own family's spending habits.

To begin with, write down under the heading "Food" all the money you have spent on food, both at home and away from home, during a one-week period. (For a monthly food-cost record, see the suggested plans in the workbook section.)

Does the amount your family spends on food in one week come to more than 24 per cent of its total expenditures for that period? If it does, it may be time to take a careful look at your food-buying habits.

Are you relying too much on frozen foods to save time and work? They certainly are convenient, but this kind of luxury can skyrocket your food budget.

Does your romantic husband impulsively decide on a "big night out" when dinner is already in the oven? Better convince him to give you a rain check, so that at least the food you've bought and cooked won't go to waste.

Another way to cut down on food expenditures might be to have only two meals a day for you and your husband on week- **17** ends at home. Tough? Well, it's easier than you think, and, remember, you gain a healthy bonus of weight loss along with the money saved. Also try having dessert after supper only every other night. And if you have a really expensive meal for a special reason, try to have an economical meal to make up for it. It can be done, and it's like money in the bank.

Now compare the other categories. How much do you spend on your home, including rent, upkeep, improvements, taxes, insurance and mortgages? What's the total? Is it more than 24 per cent of the family's spending?

List all your family's clothing costs. More than 10 per cent? How about medical and personal care? More than 9½ per cent? Are furnishings and appliances more than 5 per cent? Car and other transportation more than 15 per cent? Tobacco and alcohol more than 3½ per cent? Recreation more than 4 per cent? And so on.

If you are at all like our so-called average American family, you will probably be over the national percentage in some categories and under in others.

Wherever you are under, stay right where you are.

Where you are over (as with food or recreation, for example) take a long, hard look. Can you cut by $1 a week? Two dollars a week? If you can save $2 a week in two basic expense categories, in one year you will have magically produced $208 that you didn't have before.

Give your imagination wings. Cut costs $3 a week in these categories. Results? You'll have $312 for a color TV set or a long sight-seeing trip with your family or a down payment on a trailer.

There's a whole world of expenses that you can chop away—provided you look for ways to economize and make it a point not to take each expense for granted.

For example, the most obvious way to contend with many household leaks, literal and figurative, is to "do it yourself." There is little need to call a plumber for a simple job. The hard-**18** ware department of any store can provide good tools (and sometimes good advice) on how to tackle a given problem. Many householders have become Jacks-of-all-trades, and, with the exception of complicated jobs, they can fill in for a carpenter, a painter or a mechanic.

A recent survey showed that the average American adult male performed household chores that could cost him about $51 a week, a startling $2,652 annually. The figures are based on hourly rates in today's labor market.

Even involved projects can be taken on without calling in outside help. "How-to" books abound in libraries and on paperback counters and are available at small cost from the United States Government Printing Office. The purchase of practical, well-made tools for upkeep purposes should be considered a wise investment. A note of caution, though: *Hire that expert if you don't have the time, tools and textbooks.*

Other areas where money can be more carefully corralled are in those unseen expenses—taxes, life insurance and savings. Let's look at a few of these.

Taxes

You must pay your taxes. There's no avoiding this necessity of life. But you need not pay more than your share. To keep your income-tax costs down, for instance, there are two things you can do:

You can get tax advice. Of course, if all your income is from your salary and you rent rather than own your place, you'll have no real problem in filling out your tax return. And your Internal Revenue office may help you with uninvolved computations. But once your tax life gets complicated—you have side-line income from a business of your own that demands you use the family car; your house suffers a casualty loss; you contribute to the support of a mother-in-law—you'll do best to hire a tax specialist. Beware of the man who hangs out a shingle in late February proclaiming: "Tax Forms Filled Out—$10." Better find a Certified Public Accountant or get your family lawyer to help you. **19**

You can keep records to back up your expense deductions. Make a habit of marking such costs in a little notebook or on a sheet of paper when you incur them. Then toss that sheet of paper into your "Income Tax" hopper—a large envelope you keep in a bureau drawer.

Or, if you tend to be orderly about such things, keep an expense diary, entering dates, individuals entertained, expenses and their purposes, and so on. The Internal Revenue Service is impressed with any such records that can substantiate your claims, and surely you save money in figuring accurately the relatively large total of these many small expenses paid throughout a year.

Life insurance

Here we have one of the necessities of present-day life. The family breadwinner should not be without it, even if you have to squeeze the expense into your budget with a shoehorn. If the wage earner in your family dies, life insurance steps in and provides income, helping to replace the wage earner's salary.

Your question isn't "Should we?" No family situation is stable without it. Once you know that, you should ask yourself only "Which policy?" and "How much?"

Your family's wants must answer "How much?" But we can help you determine how much insurance protection you *need*.

Suppose you died today. How long will it be before your youngest child reaches 18? To illustrate, let's say your youngest is 8 years old. In the event of your death, someone will have to support him for at least 10 years.

Write down the amount of take-home pay you're receiving each month. From that subtract the monthly benefits husband or wife will get from social security. Let's say they come to $200 a month (you also have a 12-year-old daughter). Remember, too, to take into account your customary expenses for clothes, food, hobbies, travel, the education of your children. Your answer is the monthly "salary" someone must get **20** from life insurance for the next 10 years, if your family is to continue to live in the style to which it has become accustomed.

Then subtract from this required monthly salary figure the monthly income that your family would receive during these 10 years from social security and your present insurance policy. The figure which remains is the amount of coverage you're lacking.

Now you're fairly well prepared to call in an insurance representative to discuss making up the gap in your protection. You probably won't be oversold, now that you're armed with the specific facts and figures. Here are the three basic policies you will be offered:

Straight life policy. This is the most widely used of all types of ordinary life insurance and costs less annually than other kinds of lifetime protection. The premium is paid until you die, unless you let the dividends accumulate, which shortens the period of premium payments.

Limited-payment life. Premiums are paid on such policies only for a specified length of time—say, 30 years. Because fewer premiums are paid, each premium is larger than the comparable premium for straight life.

Term insurance. Such policies are bought for protection over a specified length of time and have no cash values, as do some other policies, and no loan privileges. However, in the early years when a young family needs protection most, term insurance costs about half as much as straight life insurance. A man with young children, who is beginning a career with prospects of an increasing income, may wish to consider this type of life insurance. If he dies while the insurance is in effect, his beneficiary collects fully.

Endowment policy. There are many other kinds of insurance policies. Many young people, for example, find the idea of an endowment policy an attractive one. This policy is a kind of savings plan, which calls for regular payment of premiums over a specified period of time. In this way you accumulate a fund, which becomes available at some future date stipulated in the policy. It can be used for the children's college education, pay- **21** ing off a mortgage, setting up a retirement fund or whatever. At the same time the policy will pay off the full amount of its face value in the event of your death. Thus, the endowment policy is both protection and a useful way to supplement your regular savings.

Of course, the best way to explore all these various types of insurance and see what application they have to your needs is to get a good insurance agent. You'll find that he can play a crucial role in your family affairs throughout your life. He will be able to analyze your situation and explain all sorts of seemingly complicated terms, like "double indemnity" (an additional sum equal to the face value of a life-insurance policy, payable if death is accidental), annuities, beneficiaries, dividends. He will also be able to tell you the advantage of paying a premium annually rather than monthly and give you other important insurance information.

And while we're on the subject, let us emphasize at this point how crucial it is for all of us, no matter how young we may be, to have a will. It's a simple matter to arrange a will. See your banker or insurance agent for advice; be sure to have a lawyer draw it for you. Much confusion, misunderstanding and real tragedy can be averted by the existence of a clearly stated will. The care of children, the disposition of money, property, personal effects—these are all vitally important matters, which cannot be left to chance in the event of your death, however remote that possibility may seem to you now.

Savings

There are some people who will argue that savings aren't essential. Whether or not the concept of savings is accepted universally as a necessity of life doesn't matter one whit. Savings *are* necessary.

Let's say you were unable to work for three months. That's a long time to be without a salary. You might get workmen's compensation benefits. You might even be paid by your employer for that three-month absence—perhaps at a lower rate.

But, then again, you might find yourself with no income. How would it affect you if you suddenly had no salary coming in and no prospect of one for at least three months? How would you pay the rent or mortgage? Who would pay for utilities? How long would the druggist wait for his money?

If you could draw on savings in the bank, then your problem would not be as serious. Savings can spell the difference between despair and hope during an unforeseen black period.

It is easier to save more by starting early and saving small amounts than by trying belatedly to save big. Whatever the amount, set aside regularly a specific sum, preferably from each pay.

Regular saving is another must in your money management planning. If you have a goal, it is much easier to save. Once you've reached your first target and have accumulated an emergency fund equal to three months' salary, you can focus on college educations, save a sizeable down payment for a car or a house, or save towards a long-dreamed-of trip. All this time your money is working for you—accumulating interest!

It's important to note, when comparing banks advertising the same interest rate, that your money will accumulate maximum interest if you put it in a bank where interest is compounded semiannually or quarterly, rather than just once a year. This will be obvious, if we stop to consider that every time interest is compounded, the amount is added to whatever you have in the savings account. The next time, interest is figured on the original amount plus the interest accumulated. It stands to reason, therefore, that the more times interest is added to the principal, the greater the total amount in your account.

What bankers call "days of grace"—where provided—can also help you gain maximum interest on your savings. Many banks pay interest on savings only when the money has been in the account for the entire interest-paying period, whether it be a year, six months or three months. Days of grace, however, allow you to be "late" in depositing your savings, without losing your interest privilege. Typically, such days of grace permit you to **23** deposit money up to the 10th day of the interest-paying period and still have it qualify as though deposited on the first of the month—a good leeway if you happen to be out of town or have forgotten to make your regular deposit.

"Interest from day of deposit" is also a real benefit. If you put your savings in a bank after the interest period has begun or after the days of grace have expired, you may not earn any interest on that money until the start of the next interest period. But some banks either pay interest from day of deposit—no matter when that day is—or pay interest beginning the first day of the month after you have made a deposit, and many pay interest to the date of withdrawal.

There are now two major ways you can save at your bank: The conventional passbook account, already discussed, and the new system of savings bonds or savings certificates.

Savings bonds work very much like government bonds. One simply purchases them, usually in amounts of $1,000 or more. After a period of time, generally two years or more, they can be redeemed with interest accumulated at a higher rate than ordinary passbook savings. The money can be withdrawn at any time before the ordinary maturity date, but in this event there is a penalty in the form of a reduced interest rate. Thus, savings bonds do give greater returns, but in most cases more initial money and a longer period of deposit are required. If you're in a situation where you may have to withdraw money quickly at any time, savings bonds are not for you. If, however, you are fortunate enough to have some extra cash and are sure you won't be needing it for some time, then savings bonds are an excellent means to get a greater return than the ordinary savings account rate of interest permits.

All these factors must be considered and discussed with your banker, if you are to put your financial house in order.

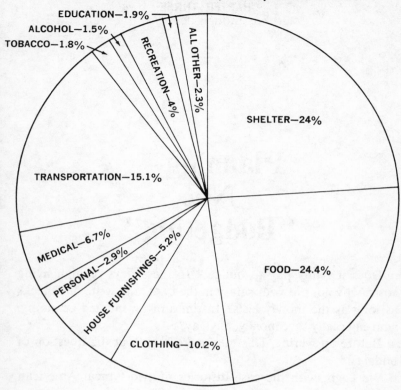

AVERAGE AMERICAN FAMILY'S SPENDING HABITS
based on statistics compiled by the Department of Labor

EDUCATION—1.9%
ALCOHOL—1.5%
TOBACCO—1.8%
RECREATION—4%
ALL OTHER—2.3%
SHELTER—24%
TRANSPORTATION—15.1%
MEDICAL—6.7%
PERSONAL—2.9%
HOUSE FURNISHINGS—5.2%
FOOD—24.4%
CLOTHING—10.2%

Shelter: Rent, mortgage payments, taxes, property insurance, gas, electricity, water, telephone, repairs and maintenance

Food: Both at home and away from home

Medical: Insurance, doctor's fees, drugs and medicines, hospital bills

Personal: Haircuts, cosmetics, beauty parlor

House furnishings: Furniture, appliances, equipment

Transportation: Automobile, insurance, commuting, long-distance travel

Recreation: TV, hobbies, toys, vacation, entertainment, hi-fi

Education: Tuition, books, newspapers, magazines

All other: Personal life insurance, gifts and contributions, interest on loans, allowances

CHAPTER THREE

Planning— Not "Budgeting"

Does it really pay to budget? In these days of high living costs, why not put your salary in the bank and write out checks as long as the money lasts? In times of an inflated economy, who can really save money, anyway?

Before answering, let's take a fresh look at the question of budgets.

We begin with the case histories of two typical American families—the Emersons and the Parks. The names are fictitious, but the events are true to life, down to the last decimal point.

A disastrous success story

The Emersons are Harry and Gladys. Harry is a young man on the way up. He is a design engineer for a large plant in the Midwest. Harry believes that the road to the top is paved with certain symbols—a nice home in which to entertain, parties that are remembered and talked about, at least for the rest of the weekend, and an attractive wife.

Harry has, he thinks, a modern attitude toward marriage. His wife is a partner, not a servant. At the end of their two-week
26 honeymoon, Harry announced firmly that he was turning the

management of the family money over to his wife.

"My job is to bring the pay checks home," he told her. "But you're the one who buys the food and furniture, so you keep the books and pay the bills. O.K.?"

Dutifully, Gladys agreed. She knew next to nothing about financial planning, but she had been to college (where, incidentally, she took only academic courses), and she knew that her friends, her parents and her parents' friends all had checking and savings accounts and life insurance. If they could manage, why couldn't she? A conscientious woman, as well as a loving wife, Gladys undertook to cope with the family income and outgo.

The Emersons might have kept their heads above the financial waters indefinitely, even though Harry, unencumbered with responsibility for keeping their checkbook in balance, went on periodic buying sprees. It wasn't to satisfy some stifled craving from boyhood, but to improve the family image. That, for instance, was the reason for the new hi-fi.

"We don't want any of that packaged junk in our living room," he explained. "We want the real components, everything balanced."

Everything did balance, too, except the checking account, of course. Gladys was hardly prepared for the bill for their new stereo system—$950.89!

Nevertheless, it wasn't until Harry's two big promotions that they were really in trouble. His salary jumped from $8,200 to $10,000, and then to $12,500. His take-home pay was now $835 a month. Who, with an income like that, couldn't afford to move to the suburbs? Well, the Emersons, as it turned out.

Shortly after Gladys knew she was going to have a baby, Harry announced that they were going to have to buy a $20,000, 5-year-old house in a suburb. Although he had no savings, he also had no long-term debts. He was able to negotiate a VA mortgage (sometimes called a G.I. mortgage) without making a down payment—but he was committed by the terms to making mortgage payments of $160 a month for thirty years, to cover principal, interest, taxes and insurance.

In the next two years, doing all the things that he felt were required to maintain his position, Harry furnished a living room, den and recreation room. In every case, he made a small down payment on the furnishings and borrowed the rest. His entertainment expenses were paid for in cash out of his current income.

On the day Harry's furniture and rugs were repossessed, he had racked up $8,254 in debts:

$1,560—owed for improvements to the kitchen
and two bathrooms
375—owed for storm windows
2,100—owed for furniture
800—owed for rugs
185—owed to the oil company for gasoline
(Harry commuted 40 miles each day)
1,800—owed on a car installment loan
675—owed to doctor and hospital
280—owed to the gardener who landscaped the property
319—owed to a men's clothing store
85—owed to another clothing store
45—owed to the electric company for service
30—owed for new stove payment

Each month, in an attempt to keep every bill collector happy, Gladys had been paying a small amount on each of the outstanding debts. In the 12 months preceding the foreclosure on the furniture, these stopgap payments added up to $517 a month. On top of that, Gladys still had $695 in regular monthly living expenses to cope with. Thus, her monthly fixed costs were $1,212. Harry's take-home pay was still $835—some $377 below those fixed costs. For the past year, then, the Emersons had been spending $377 more than they earned each month.

Harry Emerson had had no idea that he was virtually insol-
28 vent. Everything at the job was going well. He had a host of

friends who constantly told him what excellent taste he had in food, liquor and home decor. Gladys, caught in the middle between irate creditors and a husband who thought she was doing fine, had hoped for the best.

"After all," she later confided to a financial counselor, "Harry made $12,500 a year!"

Harry Emerson, an honorable man, dug in his heels and refused to file a personal bankruptcy suit. Instead, he chose to sell his $20,000 house.

He and Gladys moved in with Gladys' mother. Harry took a "moonlighting" job to speed up repayment of his creditors. Gladys was unable to work; her ulcer (perhaps the result of those months of worrying about debts) prohibited it. In the years that followed, Harry Emerson, a man who "earned a good living," no longer went on spending sprees.

Too much of a good thing

Now, let's take up the case of Ruth and John Park, both 28 years old. The Parks have one child, a 3-year-old daughter. John earns $6,500 as a draftsman. Ruth does not work.

The Parks' financial problem began one evening when Ruth announced during supper—without warning—that she and John were going on a budget. "Why?" John wanted to know. Because it was high time, she explained. A threatening letter from a collection agency had arrived in the morning mail, coupled with an irate phone call that afternoon from a department store, both demanding payment within five days. The status of their bills, she said, was "horrible and embarrassing." They would be bankrupt or out on the street with all their belongings within a month.

Because of her extreme anxiety over even minor bills, Ruth quite understandably sought security in a budget. And, in keeping with such anxiety, she was determined to make her budget ironclad—for only then would she live in what she considered complete safety.

The truth of the Parks' financial situation was this: The **29**

Parks did need a budget, because John Park tended to go overboard on buying household gadgets as "surprises" and taking his wife to expensive restaurants, where he often ran up a $30 bill. Moreover, the Parks should have set up a savings program. Still, they were by no means on the brink of financial catastrophe.

That decisive night, Ruth Park vowed that she and her husband would toe the line in this perilous world of domestic finance. So in subsequent days she doled out 25 cents here and $1.29 there (in keeping with the budget she'd clipped from a women's magazine). Ruth hacked at their expenses in this manner: She cut her $75-a-month food bill down to $38, eliminated entertainment completely and limited their nightly cocktails to one each on Saturday nights.

True to her word, in the next six months Ruth held the family unrelentingly to the budget. It was touch and go at times. The car suddenly needed a $55 valve job; John had to have a tooth extracted, $15, and they had to buy a $15 (secondhand) bed for their daughter. To make up for such unanticipated expenses, Ruth had to juggle the budget, and juggle she did. Consequently, there were days when, for example, John's haircut money had to be spent for gasoline—not a haircut.

While John and Ruth suffered through the financial aspects of their impossible budget, they fared even less well in their human relations.

By the end of the first month, every conversation they had seemed to be about money.

"Why can't you eat a sandwich and a cup of coffee?" Ruth would demand. "Why do you have to have a big meal in the middle of the day? Don't I feed you at home?" And off she'd go to sulk.

By the middle of the third month, John was frustrated. "Can't we reach some sort of compromise on the budget?" he asked. He thought he was being tactful.

"You mean compromise on our lives," Ruth said. "A compromise that will put a hole in the dike. Well, we don't need a compromise. We need a *man* who can live within the bounds of his own financial abilities."

Their daughter's crying in the bedroom ended this conversation, but similar ones followed.

When four months had passed, Ruth and John no longer talked about the budget. They fought about it.

"Why don't you go out and earn more money if you don't like what I'm doing?" she shouted.

By the sixth month, the budget was obviously running the family. A bill collector called Ruth that morning and she hit the ceiling. She had made out the check the week before. That night, when her husband came home, and before he had his overcoat off, she screamed, "Isn't it bad enough that you can't support your family? Couldn't you at least remember to mail the checks I gave you last week? Jerome's called today for their money, and I felt like an idiot. What did you do with the check?"

John later told his lawyer—while arranging for a separation —that he'd had it "up to here," pointing at his throat with a jabbing motion.

Common sense and sensible budgeting

The lesson to be learned from these case histories is clear. Both the Emersons and the Parks were dead wrong in the way they managed their finances. The Emersons were sorely in need of a monthly financial record, and, as the Parks learned, a strait-jacket budget can be worse than no budget at all.

Specifically, a family that makes no plan for the financial future will court ultimate disaster, for no man can escape the shadow of the bill collector forever. At the other extreme, the family that sticks rigidly to a budget, come hell or high water, takes the zest out of living—and love out of living, too.

How do you feel now about the budgeting question?

Your answer may be along these lines: "I certainly don't want to wind up like Harry Emerson. So I guess we should plan our expenses and keep track of what we owe. But I want no part **31** of budgeting for budgeting's sake. Let's face it. We want to live, too!"

If you do subscribe to that middle-of-the-road approach, you've made a wise decision. Yours is the answer given by seasoned family counselors.

What, you may ask, is a sensible budget? First, it's a personal road map for financial living. Think of the budget as organized spending and saving drawn up ahead of time—not afterward.

Second, a sensible budget is one geared to *your* family's way of living. Your plan should fit the needs and objectives of *your* household, not your neighbor's—even if your neighbor earns exactly as much as you and has just as many kids.

Why can't two plans ever be alike? Because while families on the surface may appear to be similar, those families—when looked at just a little more closely—are drastically different. Here are two quick examples of how we all differ, even on such simple things as our needs for recreation and food.

You and your family, say, enjoy going to the country for two weeks every summer. When you get there you like to live it up. So you spend $400 a year on vacation, and you enjoy every penny of it.

Your neighbor, on the other hand, has decided to forego his vacations for several years. Instead, he works around his home and puts away money for the two bedrooms he plans to add to his house. So your neighbor, who earns as much as you and has as many children, has no vacation allotment in his budget. But he does have a yearly $300 sum set aside for home expansion, while your family has no such home-expansion savings.

Here's another example that proves that no two families are alike: Your family enjoys good food—lots of it. You eat sirloin steaks and serve wine with the meal. Your neighbors—the family earning as much as you—couldn't care less about fancy food. They eat stews, meat loaf, hamburgers and sometimes have a glass of beer. The upshot: Your neighbor's family spends one-third less on food and 50 per cent less on liquor.

32   Obviously, then, you and your neighbors could never swap budgets. And that observation has been made on the basis of just two or three items in a budget. Closer examination would reveal eight or nine different basic approaches to money spending between you and the neighboring family.

A sensible budget, as a third characteristic, is one that's reached by agreement between both husband and wife. *A budget won't work when only one member of the family wants to budget. It takes two to budget!* You'll also do well to let the children participate in the areas that concern them.

Psychologically, the odds are all in your favor whenever you enlist—not demand—the help of others. After all, the children's activities and needs will be affected by this thing they hear discussed so much—"the budget." And your level-headed approach may set a good example for them in later life.

Fourth, a sensible budget gives you a chance to think about alternative living plans. It lets you see those alternatives more clearly, helps you to weigh values and to make wise decisions. In short, a sensible budget helps you to put first things first, to stay within your income and to avoid hopeless entanglements in debt and financial worries.

How do we begin?

Now we come to the big question: How do you go about setting up a sensible budget?

There are several ways you can handle the job. You might do well to experiment with a few until you find one that works best for you. To get you started, we'll give you the details of one very simple but adequate budgeting plan. If it appeals to you, try it.

You'll notice that in this plan you don't have to hold yourself to 25 per cent of total income for food, and 30 per cent of income for shelter. It isn't that kind of budget. On the contrary, it's a sensible one, especially for families budgeting their expenses for the first time. It is designed to help you build up a savings account, meet your fixed expenses, pay your day-to-day living costs, and establish a reserve fund to pay for a new roof **33** on your house or the repair of a water heater in the basement.

Quite naturally, neither this plan nor any other will enable you to live beyond your means. If your take-home pay is $600 a month, you will not be able to spend $615 a month.

To start your plan of organized spending, convert your take-home pay into terms of *monthly* income. If you're paid monthly, there's no problem. If you're paid semimonthly, multiply one pay check by two. If you're paid every two weeks, multiply your take-home pay by 26 (number of two-week periods in a year) and then divide that answer by 12 (months). If you're paid weekly, multiply your take-home pay by 52 (number of pay periods), then divide by 12. You now know how much money you have to spend—and to save—every month.

Your next step is vital. Determine how much money you want to save. A sound beginning is to put aside the first 5 per cent of income.

Now make a list of all your monthly fixed expenses. In our center worksheet section we have included a sample list of monthly expenses. You may wish to be guided by that list or perhaps to make yours more detailed—for example, it may help you to break down your "Clothing" allotment into "Purchases" and "Upkeep" (cleaning, laundering, repairing); under "Household" you may wish to show repairs, cleaning supplies, household help, etc.

You now have a subtotal of your fixed monthly expenses. To get the total, you'll need to make up one more list of fixed expenses that are usually due on a less than once-a-month basis.

Taxes
Homeowner insurance
Life insurance (paid other than monthly)
Car insurance
Car registration and licenses

Perhaps your insurance premiums fall due quarterly or annu-
34 ally, and you pay real estate taxes every six months. Add up

those fixed, but less frequent, expenses, and divide the total by 12. Now you know what those expenses cost you on a monthly basis.

Add that total to the subtotal you already have of fixed expenses. Your answer in dollars and cents will tell you how much money you must put aside monthly to meet your fixed expenses.

To make our explanation as clear as possible, we'll assume that your monthly take-home pay is $500, you've decided to save $25 a month (5 per cent), and you must pay out $300 in fixed expenses. You now have $175 to work with every month.

Figure out what your flexible or—for a better name—your day-to-day living costs are. In this list you'll put such items (along with their costs to you) as: laundry, church contributions, gifts, recreation, dry cleaning, medicine and newspapers and magazines. Once you've completed this list (and it's wise to be thorough now), you'll know what your total day-to-day costs are on a monthly basis.

To carry out our illustration, we'll say that such costs total $125 a month for your family. The remainder—$50 in this case—should be earmarked for future unforeseen expenses.

On the following pages we have presented another method of family budgeting, and in the center section there are more worksheets for your own use.

Your bank and your budget

You have just a few more things to do before launching your budget: Set up a savings account, if you do not already have one, for your monthly savings plan; set up a checking account for your fixed expenses only (don't put any other funds in this account); set up a separate checking account for your day-to-day living costs.

You can modify this budget plan in a number of ways to suit your needs. You may prefer to pay your day-to-day living costs on a cash basis, putting the money in separate envelopes, each one labeled for its specific purpose. You may set up as **35**

An average monthly budget for family of four

Here is a sample monthly budget for a husband, wife, and their two small children (one child is 3 years old, the other is just 1). The husband's monthly take-home pay is $550. He lives with his family in the suburbs of a major American city, in a $16,000 house.

Use this budget as a guide only. It will not necessarily work for you, but it may help you to develop a similar budget.

The family keeps a record of its monthly expenditures on a form similar to the one reproduced below. Thus, as an expense is paid for, the outlay is recorded in the proper category.

payment date	savings $ 10	shelter $100	food $100	house-hold $ 50	heat $ 30	utilities $ 20	clothing $ 25
1	10	100	30				
8			25	20			
12			16		30		10
18			14	9		20	
20				9			
27			15				
TOTAL	$ 10	$100	$100	$ 38	$ 30	$ 20	$ 10
carry f'w'd	—	—	—	$ 12	—	—	$ 15

That way it is easy for both husband and wife to see at a glance when and where they have spent their monthly allotment.

In the example given below, you will note that the family spent only $7 for entertainment this month—not the allotted $15. Thus they have $8 left over for entertainment to add to next month's budget, giving them $23 to spend on entertainment that month. If, by chance, the family overspends in any one category, the deficit is subtracted from the next month's allotment and the family is protected from going in the red longer than one month.

medical $ 15	life insurance $ 20	car maintenance $ 20	car insurance $ 10	car payment $ 45	entertainment $ 15	misc. $ 90
	20		10			9
		6				25
				45	7	20
		6				17
15		6				4
$ 15	$ 20	$ 18	$ 10	$ 45	$ 7	$ 75
—	—	$ 2	—	—	$ 8	$ 15

many categories—or as few—as you feel comfortable with. And you may, if you wish, operate your budget on a weekly or a semimonthly basis as well.

The main point of this is, of course, to get you to organize your spending. Now you know where your money goes, how far it must stretch, where you can cut down. Since your take-home pay, and your family's tastes and goals are unique and unlike your neighbor's, you can see why arbitrary budgets do not work. There are no precise figures or percentages which fit you and your family.

To keep a spending plan running smoothly it is wise to discuss it in detail with your husband, or wife, and arrange some simple way to keep the record up-to-date. In this way you can locate money leaks and see that you're making your money go where you want it to. You'll undoubtedly discover that your expenditures diminish in some areas, as they increase in others.

The actual record can be kept in a notebook with ruled columns, or you may find that a chart (like the one in the workbook section) is more useful.

Foremost in making this plan work is family co-operation. Keep the budget record in a convenient place. Perhaps one person can be responsible for listing the family expenditures at a specific time, once a week. Then everyone can see what's covered or omitted next pay check. Make notations, if necessary. The children should have a share in deciding what some of the family goals are, too.

The main spending decisions are generally made jointly by husband and wife, who should understand that slipping over one month will mean dipping into the reserves the next. Such an overshot usually can be regained in the immediate months ahead. But if the expenditures continue to exceed income, it's time to reappraise together, bearing in mind that a budget of this sort is flexible.

CHAPTER FOUR

Tips on Borrowing

With an adequate fistful of dollars, anyone can take a trip around the world, buy an airplane, a Picasso painting or, in fact, any salable item. If all of us, then, had an inexhaustible supply of money, there'd be far less need for financial management.

But life is not quite like that. Most of us work for so many dollars a year—a set sum. Sometimes both marriage partners contribute to annual income. And sometimes extra jobs or investments in the stock market and real estate add to our annual basic earnings. Whatever the sources, there is a limit on the amount of money any one of us receives in any one year. And there are inevitably times in our lives—even in the lives of those of us who manage our money wisely—when we need more money than we have on hand. Then we find it necessary to borrow.

The all-important credit rating

Whether or not we succeed in borrowing money, and in borrowing the amount we seek, is another matter. The chief factor that determines whether or not we will be able to borrow money, and how much money any lender will let us have, **39** is our credit rating. If we have a good credit rating—that is, if we've paid our bills regularly—chances are that we'll have no trouble in getting a reasonable loan. And, depending upon the amount of our income, we'll be able to borrow anywhere from $100 to $100,000.

So it is important to know what constitutes a good credit rating. There are five main factors. Some of the more important points that a bank's lending officer looks at before he decides whether or not you are a good credit risk are:

Previous loans. Have you ever paid off a loan before? If so, chalk up a plus mark in your favor. Banks believe that anyone who has repaid a loan promptly before will repay the next loan, too. Of course, if you've defaulted on a loan, been sued or had to have some item repossessed in order for the lending institution to collect from you, you'll have a poor credit rating.

Present charge accounts. Do you pay your monthly charge accounts at department stores with reasonable regularity? If so, that too is a plus mark in your favor. All a bank actually wants to know is: Are you capable of repaying a loan in the time allotted and are you willing to?

Home ownership. Do you own your own home? Or have you lived at the same apartment for a long time? If you can answer yes to either question, give yourself another plus. Such things as home ownership or continued residence at one apartment show the bank that you're a stable individual.

Steady employment record. Have you worked for the same company (not necessarily in the same office or plant) for five, 10 or 15 years? Just as with home ownership, stability of employment constitutes another plus factor. On the other hand, if you've been with a company for only a matter of weeks or months, make it a point to explain that you worked —if such is the case—for your previous employer for five, 10 or more years. Banks realize that individuals change jobs from time to time to improve themselves, but it's up to you to show the bank that you are not an irresponsible job-hopper.

40 *Bank accounts.* Do you have a savings account or a checking account—or both? Good! If they are at the bank where you're seeking a loan, so much the better. It's not necessary, of course, but it does help to borrow where you are known.

If you pass muster on these five points—or, in some instances, on three of them—you should wind up with a good credit rating.

Banks do look differently, and usually kindly, on young adults who haven't had time to establish a good credit rating only because they haven't made any loans or bought anything on the installment plan. For such newcomers to the financial markets, banks will concentrate on the young adult's family background, residence, education and the job he presently holds. Banks want to establish good relations with such promising young people, not only to make new customers, but to begin what they hope will be a profitable long-term relationship.

Here are some of the negative factors that will kill your credit rating outright in the eyes of the lending officer as you sit at his desk discussing a loan:

An inability to identify yourself. Most banks will consider any one of a score of identification items, including driver's licenses, birth certificates, union cards, social security cards, draft cards, hospitalization cards, receipted bills or correspondence from responsible companies, and legal documents.

A relatively impermanent address. A residence that is a rooming house, a hotel, a furnished room, a post-office box or an address in care of a friend is suspect. Perhaps you can furnish proof of previous long residence in one place.

An applicant whose employment is extremely unsteady or unreliable: for example, an actor who is out of work a good deal of the time or a stock car racer whose earnings are of an unpredictable nature.

An application made at a bank which is quite distant from your residence.

An applicant who is under age and has no parent or "sponsor" to help repay the loan. **41**

An applicant who stands to be drafted before his loan will be repaid. Quite obviously he is not as sound a credit risk because of his new "employer." Such an applicant may need a cosponsor or cosigner who will guarantee that the loan will be repaid.

How strong is your credit rating?

So much for establishing a credit rating. Now let's look at the strength of your credit rating. It's on the strength of your rating that the bank determines how much money it will lend you. The stronger the credit rating, the more money will be made available to you.

Probably the biggest single factors the bank will look at in this regard are your salary and any investment income you may have. The more you earn, the more you'll be able to borrow.

If you're earning $2,000 a year—as an obviously exaggerated example—the bank will turn you down flat. Why? Because at today's prices you can't possibly meet current expenses and repay a bank loan on such a subminimum salary. But if your salary is $5,000 a year or higher, you stand a good chance of getting a loan from the bank.

Another factor will be the nature of your job. If your employment is on a day-to-day basis, or if it is highly insecure—as, say, an actor whose show may close any night—these matters will also be considered and carefully weighed.

After your income picture, the bank will consider your living expenses. Consider this: Both Mr. A and Mr. B earn $9,000 a year. Mr. A, however, is married, has six children and an expensive home. Mr. B is not married and does not contribute to the support of anyone other than himself; he lives in a small apartment in the city near his work. Who, then, in your estimation stands a better chance of repaying the debt? Of course, Mr. B is the better risk, based on the facts we've presented.

42   Not only, then, is the bank interested in your earnings, it is also interested in your expenses. Are you already overextended in installment debt? If so, the bank may be hesitant.

The simplest way to find out how much your bank will lend you is to go and ask.

One way to borrow is to take a loan against something of value that you own. This "something" is called collateral. Examples are your car—if fully paid—real estate, common or preferred stocks, bonds, savings-account passbooks and the cash-surrender value of life-insurance policies.

Why does collateral help? Because it minimizes the risk the bank would otherwise have to take. For example, suppose you want to borrow $2,000 for one year. You earn $9,000 a year, have a family of four children and have to make installment payments of $86 a month on a previous loan. Under such circumstances you might not get the $2,000 loan, because you'd have more debts than you could afford.

But if you owned $3,000 worth of common stock and put it up as collateral, the bank would lend you the $2,000. The reasoning is this: If you fail to repay the loan, the bank will sell the stock, collect whatever is due on the loan and then give the rest of the money to you. It is important to remember, however, that collateral is usually used when circumstances do not dictate an ordinary unsecured loan.

Another financial device for borrowing money which may substitute for collateral is to use what is called a "comaker." A comaker, or cosigner, is simply someone who signs a note agreeing to pay off your loan in the event that you are unable to complete payments. A young person applying for a loan may find that the bank will ask if a relative or friend will be a comaker for his note. This provides the bank with added insurance that if such a young man or woman simply can't make the payments, another person—one that is known to be financially solvent—will be responsible.

Since the money you borrow must be returned, the act of borrowing money is quite the same as renting a car, a power saw or an apartment. You pay for the use of the bank's **43** money. In this case, the rent you pay is called interest.

The amount of interest you'll pay on any one loan depends in large measure on (1) the type of loan you are taking, and (2) from whom you borrow the money.

Borrowing money in different ways

To show you the many ways you can borrow money, let's go on an extensive shopping tour for the $1,000 you need. We'll assume that you're employed, have been living in the same home with your family for four years and have no major debts.

First, we will visit your insurance company. Here you can borrow money against any insurance policy you own that has accumulated cash-surrender values. Typically, policies such as straight life, limited-payment life, and endowments have such cash-value reserves. Term-insurance policies do not.

A loan against your insurance policy has two major advantages: (1) You get the money in a matter of days with no questions asked, no credit check made on you, and (2) the rate of interest may be low. The specific interest rate that you'll pay is written into your insurance policy. If you took out the policy before 1939, the rate is probably 6 per cent a year; if you bought the policy after 1939, the rate is about 5 per cent a year, and if you have a VA-insurance policy, the rate is 4 per cent a year.

Under the terms of this loan, you'll be allowed to keep the money you've borrowed as long as you want. And you can repay the loan in any fashion convenient to you: in one lump sum, in monthly installments, in semiannual payments or in any system you choose. But in that freedom lies one disadvantage: For every year that you keep the money, you must pay another round of interest—4 per cent, 5 per cent or 6 per cent of the money still owed. So while such loans are relatively inexpensive on a one-year basis, they can be costly —as any loan can—when spread over a number of years.

44   Another—and somewhat smaller—drawback: If you should die while the loan is in effect, the insurance company from whom you've borrowed the money will subtract the amount of the loan from the face amount of the policy. The remainder will be sent to your beneficiary.

For the purposes of our little tour of money-lending sources, let's assume that all of your policies are term policies, and thus you cannot borrow your needed $1,000 from this worthwhile—when properly used—source.

The next place to look in our search for a $1,000 loan is the mortgage on your house.

Suppose you've paid off $8,000 of your $20,000 mortgage. That means you owe $12,000 on the mortgage. You can, if you wish, take out a new mortgage on the house for, say, $15,000. That way you'd get $3,000 in cash—the difference between your new mortgage and what you owed on the old mortgage.

Such refinancing is excellent for long-term borrowing of large amounts of money. But it isn't always practical for small amounts, chiefly because there are several costs involved in refinancing, such as a possible prepayment penalty on the old mortgage, and perhaps a new title search and a fee for the drawing up of a new mortgage. Moreover, since mortgage rates do go up and down, you may very well discover that you've cashed in a 6 per cent mortgage at a time when only an 8 per cent mortgage is available. Those two percentage points can make a big difference in the amount of interest you'll pay over the term of a mortgage.

The idea of refinancing, or recasting, is also applicable to personal loans. If, for example, you find yourself unable to meet the monthly repayments on a $1,000 loan with $500 left to pay, it is often possible to chop the remaining payments in half by extending them over a longer period of time. Thus, you will find yourself making payments of about $42 (plus whatever additional interest there may be) over a period of 12 months, rather than the original $88.33 a month for six months. And, if your credit is sound, an additional **45** sum may be lent to you over the original principal, thereby increasing the amount borrowed, as well as extending the period of time over which the payments are to be made. This is often called "consolidating" your debt and is a widespread practice.

There is another way to borrow that we should thoroughly explore. You can get a loan indirectly from a commercial bank to purchase an automobile, mobile home, appliance or other commodity from the dealer of your choice.

Let's see how this so-called indirect method—making an installment loan without going to the bank—works. Suppose you are buying a new car priced at $2,400. You have either cash or a car to trade in. Your down payment is $800. The dealer needs $1,600 more to complete the sale. After clearing your credit with the bank, he will ask you to sign a "Retail Installment Contract" for this amount. He then proceeds to discount, or sell, the contract to the bank.

You drive away in your new car as soon as the contract is signed and the bank says O.K. to your credit. The dealer receives his $1,600 from the bank. And the bank, in turn, will forward you a payment-coupon book and related papers. You have thus "indirectly" taken out an installment loan, without actually going to the bank itself.

Another way to borrow money, particularly in small amounts, is through a finance company. These finance, or small-loan, companies are regulated by various state laws. They usually make small loans at rates as high as 2½ to 3 per cent a month. This is, of course, considerably more than you will pay elsewhere. But small-loan credit is usually easier to get, and finance companies can take greater risks by charging this higher rate of interest.

Credit unions also are a good place to borrow small amounts of money and, in some cases, at interest rates that are comparatively low. Credit unions are formed by church groups, unions, fraternal lodges and other organizations for the precise purpose of helping out members in need of a loan. Non-members, of course, are not eligible.

The best way to borrow money

All types and sizes of loans are offered at a full–service bank. You can borrow to buy a new car or a boat. You can borrow to repair or improve your house. And you can borrow to pay taxes, go on a vacation or even to pay insurance premiums in advance. Banks are virtually "department stores" of finance. The amount available to any one individual will depend on his credit background and ability to repay.

Regardless of the type of loan you take at your bank, it will fall into one of two major categories. It will be either a single-payment loan or an installment loan. Of the two, the installment loan is by far the more popular. Here are the details on both:

Single-payment loans. These are for the most part secured loans—that is, they are made against collateral. Further, such one-payment loans may be demand loans (the time for repayment is left open, but the money owed must be paid when the bank asks for it) or time loans (the money borrowed is to be repaid on a prearranged date). Just as the name implies, a single-payment loan is repaid in one lump sum. The big disadvantage is that such loans don't provide the periodic repayment discipline that you automatically get with installment loans.

Installment loans. There are two important facts you should know about these loans: (1) The interest cost is calculated on the full amount of the loan and is generally paid in advance—bankers say "discounted"—and (2) a portion of the loan must be repaid each month during the term of the loan, which may be anywhere from 12 to 60 months.

While there are several kinds of installment loans, the "big three" are these: auto, personal and home improvement. We will discuss car loans in Chapter Five. Let's now briefly define personal and home improvement loans:

Personal loans. Only your signature, and perhaps that of a comaker or endorser, on the loan is needed when you borrow money from a bank on a personal loan. You will use such an **47** installment loan whenever you need money to meet medical or dental bills, pay state or Federal taxes, consolidate outstanding bills or buy a refrigerator or rug. Generally, $5,000 is the maximum you can borrow on this type of loan. Since the loan is made on the strength of your signature, your credit rating, quite obviously, must be good. In some cases banks do prefer more than just one signature. This is when a comaker's signature is needed.

Home-improvement loans. If you want to improve your home or repair damages, then a home-improvement loan is what you need. The bank will provide the money needed for new roofing, painting, plumbing or building on additions—any sound improvement. The outstanding characteristics of this type of loan are the length of time you have to repay the loan and the amount of money you can borrow.

Because of the obvious purpose involved here, banks treat these transactions somewhat differently.

Now that we've shopped around for money both outside and inside a bank, you can see that you'll be able to get many types of loans for worthwhile purposes at a full-service bank. You can take one, two, or perhaps three years to repay the money, too.

A special tip on borrowing

Want to know the best and least expensive way to borrow? When you need some extra money, try a low-cost loan, pledging your savings-account passbook as collateral, instead of taking the money from your savings. In this way you keep your savings account intact, and, by paying back the loan as promised, you gain a good credit rating at the bank. Also, you'll find that since the bank is assured of payment because you have pledged the amount from your savings, a low rate of interest is charged for this type of loan. Meanwhile your savings still earn interest.

Don't wait until you need a big loan to establish your credit. **48** Take steps ahead of time. Borrow a small amount and put it to good use. When repayment time arrives, go back to the bank and repay the loan plus the interest.

For young people or others who have "always paid cash," this is probably one of the best ways of establishing a good credit rating, not only at the bank, but at department stores and other places of business. (See center workbook section for worksheets to record each amount charged to various accounts per month.) You will now have a record of borrowing money and paying it back on time. If you ever really do need to borrow money in the future, that record will make it much easier for you to get the money you need.

Remember, borrowing money is not a bad practice. Done properly, it is a vital part of good money management.

In fact, paying back a loan on a regular basis is a kind of enforced savings. Instead of saving haphazardly over a long period of time, a loan provides the ability to purchase and to possess an item precisely when it is needed. Repayments then become a kind of substitute for savings. The advantage is that you own the car or house or television set all the time that you are paying off the loan. Thus, borrowing is really an excellent way to accumulate capital.

However—though you know now that money is available to responsible borrowers for worthwhile purposes, and know further that financially sophisticated people do not consider all borrowing necessarily unwise, do not run out and apply for loan unless you are completely certain it is both needed and justified. Experience has shown that many items a young wage-earner feels he "cannot live without" are not necessary, but only desirable—and not worth having until you can pay for them on your own.

It is practical, for instance, to borrow money for buying or building a house; for maintaining or improving one; for a necessary car; for education; for items, in short, that are of major worth and will continue to be so in the future. It is possible that a fur jacket or a trip to Europe may be—for you—in this category, but in general it is not wise to borrow for pure luxury. **49**

One further warning: Never allow a persistent salesman to high-pressure you into buying something you don't want, can't afford, or are perfectly willing to wait for until next year. And never, *never* sign a blank contract.

If borrowing is not done properly and wisely, financial chaos may result. Whenever you have an installment-credit problem, see your banker for his help and financial advice. Contrary to all the cartoons and sayings you may have seen in magazines, bankers would much rather help you with your money problem than repossess your property or sue for collection. Your banker is as anxious as you are to maintain your sound financial footing, so that you can do business together for many years to come.

Am I really paying 11 per cent on my loan?

In Chapter Five of this book on money management, we show you how to determine the dollar cost of a loan. Understanding the dollar-cost system—how many dollars you must pay back on a loan—is essential to effective money management.

More sophisticated students of money management want to be able to determine the so-called true *rate of interest paid on a loan. The true rate is found by determining first the simple annual rate of interest.*

Say you want to take out a loan of $1,000. Your bank tells you that the interest charge for one year is 6 per cent, or $60. That is the "simple interest" rate. However, you agree that each month for the next 12 months you will pay back to the bank $88.33. Therefore, at the end of the first month, after you make your initial $88.33 payment, the $1,000 you have borrowed is only $911.67. At the end of the second month, the $1,000 is only $823.34. Each month when you make another payment, the $1,000 is always $88.33 less than it was the preceding month. Because of these monthly payments the average amount of money you actually have for use during the one-year period is approximately $514.19. This average is calculated by taking the total face amount of the principal for each month, still in your possession, and dividing by 12.

Now it is simple to see that $60 is not 6 per cent of $514.19, the average amount of money you actually have during the period of the loan. It is, instead 11.66 per cent. And this 11.66 per cent is the true interest rate. The true interest rate is often referred to as "discount interest," since most banks discount, or deduct, the dollar cost of the loan from the face amount when the loan is made.

We must never confuse this use of the term "discount" with any implication of bargain-basement shopping. When your banker asks you if you want the interest discounted, he is not offering you any kind of special under-the-counter deal. Rather, he is asking you if you would like the $60 charge deducted in advance from the $1,000, thereby leaving you with an actual amount of $940 in your pocket and a total amount of $1,000 to repay in monthly installments of $83.33; or if you would prefer to have the $60 charge added to the loan, giving you a total of $1,000 in your pocket and the amount of $1,060 to repay in monthly installments of $88.33.

All this sounds much more complicated than it is. Explained in more simple terms, the fact is that your banker is not only charging you for the use of the money, but for the considerable amount of bookkeeping involved, not to mention the inherent risks in lending money in the first place. With all of these records and mailings and figurings to allow for—and despite the risks involved—the rate of interest remains remarkably low, and, in general, well earned!

The Truth-in-Lending law

All banks, by law, must disclose the actual interest on loans. This is one provision of the Truth-in-Lending law. Information is available at all banks.

CHAPTER FIVE

Paying for
Your Most
Important
Expenditures

Two of the most expensive things you'll ever buy in your lifetime are a house and an automobile.

Just think for a minute about the cost of a medium-priced car. Chances are it is $3,000 or more—assuming it's not a compact model and has accessories, such as radio, heater, automatic transmission, power steering and power brakes.

Think what $3,000 will get you in a department store. You can make any one of these six purchases—give or take a dollar or two—for $3,000:

30 portable TV sets	*7 color TV sets*
10 refrigerators	*3 stereo systems*
15 $200 sofas	*15 washing machines*

That list barely scratches the surface, but, short as it is, it shows that $3,000 for a car—or for anything—is a lot of money.

When you buy a house, you really leap into the "top ticket" brackets. In many areas it's not easy to buy a good house for less than $15,000. And in some suburbs surrounding big cities, you're lucky if you can find suitable housing for under $20,000.

In a word, buying a house is a serious financial undertaking.

Since the house and the car are long-term, expensive purchases, they deserve special attention. We don't intend to tell you what to look for in either home or auto construction—that's not our aim. You can find plenty of good books on both subjects. But it's up to us to see that you get the best possible financing. Let's start with the house.

How much can you afford to pay for a house?

You should know the answer to that question before you go out house hunting. Otherwise, you're going to waste your time looking at a lot of houses you won't be able to buy, no matter how nice they are. You can probably buy 1,000 different consumer items in this world, without anyone ever saying to you, "Hold on there. You can't afford this. You don't earn enough money." But just that will happen to you when you try to buy a house that's out of your reach. You won't be able to get a loan—a mortgage—to buy the house.

If you already own a home and are thinking about moving to a bigger one, then you know what that $18,000 house, say, costs you today. So you know whether or not you can move up to $22,500. But if you've never owned a home before, you'll have to do some arithmetic. And, for your own peace of mind in the years to come, you should be realistic about costs.

There are several old-time formulas you can use to find out what your total purchase price should be. And depending upon which formula you select, your answer may vary by as much as $5,000.

You'll do best, we believe, to use a conservative formula. That way you'll wind up with a house that you can more likely afford, rather than one you can barely pay for. Here's why you'll need that leeway of $1,000 or so: *There are more expenses involved in home ownership than will ever meet your eye, until you're a home owner.*

Let's say, for example, that you've bought a house with a lawn that requires reseeding, a roof that has a slight leak and **53** gutters that need replacing. Will it need painting next year? How old is the furnace? What about maintenance items, such as rakes, shovels, power mower, extension ladder? All these costs don't come up every year, but they will probably hit you with enough regularity, month in and month out, to cost you at least $300 a year.

One rule of thumb says to allow 2 per cent of the purchase price of the house for upkeep. And we've said nothing of rising real estate taxes—taxes you'll have to pay, with few or no discounts ever given. You stand a better chance of meeting total costs if you buy a house with a safety margin.

The best way to arrive at a conservative estimate of how much you can afford to pay for a house is to work with take-home pay totals, not gross income. The formula we suggest is simplicity itself: Multiply your annual take-home pay by 2½, if you have less than four children. The answer you get is a conservative, but reasonable, estimate of how much you can afford to pay for a house.

Of course, there are many other things to consider when looking for a house, particularly if it is your first one. Let's take, for example, the case history of the Rider family, Joe and Martha, and their two small children. The Riders had been living in a four-room city apartment since their marriage, but as the children grew older and approached school age, Joe and Martha decided to buy a house and move to the suburbs. Deciding on a small community within easy distance of the city, they began, with the help of a local real estate agent, to look at various houses in the neighborhood.

The agent showed them several fine homes that were currently for sale. One especially caught their fancy: a modern, two-story house with plenty of land around it.

"It's only a five-minute walk to school," Martha said. "And you can drive to the train station in less than half an hour."

The agent also pointed out the beautiful neighborhood and the fine quality of the house's construction.

54   "We're definitely interested," Joe said. "How much?"

"$35,000," the agent replied.

Thirty-five thousand dollars! This was almost twice the amount the Riders had calculated they could afford. "We'd better take a look at something else," they said.

Eventually, they settled on a slightly older home, farther from the center of town, that cost only $20,000. Such adjustments to the reality of your financial situation can be made without compromising any of your family's real needs. In this case, Martha enjoyed decorating the older house in her own style, the children were bussed to school, Joe left earlier for the train and they all lived happily ever after.

Do you need a mortgage?

A mortgage is a loan you get from any one of several lending sources—including commercial banks—to buy a house. People generally borrow the greater share of the purchase price. Their own cash is called their down payment or equity.

A mortgage is probably the biggest and the longest-term loan you'll ever take out in your life. The interest rate on this loan or mortgage varies by geographic area. The rate for new mortgages being granted also varies from time to time, depending on a number of economic factors in effect when you apply for your mortgage. The range of mortgage rates over the past two decades has been roughly 4 per cent to just under 9 per cent. You will need a mortgage, unless you have a sufficient sum and are willing to spend it all to buy your house outright.

Mortgages are generally repaid monthly in equal installments. The amount you pay each month usually includes money to pay off the principal and money to pay the interest on the loan. In the early years of the mortgage, a higher proportion of the money pays the interest. So, if your monthly mortgage payment totals $126, at first the interest portion of that money may be as high as $100 and the principal portion the remaining $26. As the years go by, the situation reverses itself. Finally, out of every $126 in monthly payments, as much as $125 will be applied to the principal and only $1 toward the interest.

It's been the practice in recent years to make home-ownership budgeting as painless as possible by including a monthly portion of annual real estate taxes and fire-insurance costs in each mortgage payment. That way you're not suddenly hit with these costs all at once.

How big a mortgage should you get?

To answer the question, you'll have to do more arithmetic. Write down the amount you have decided you can afford to pay for a house (2 or 2½ times your annual take-home pay). We'll say $18,000 as an illustration. Now write down the amount of money you've saved for this home-buying venture. Let's say $5,000. Now, from your $5,000 savings, subtract $1,000 to cover closing costs and moving expenses. Your banker can give you a reasonably accurate closing-cost figure— the money you'll need for lawyers' fees, Federal documentary stamps, fire-insurance premiums and real estate taxes.

At the formal closing, you should be represented by your lawyer, who will explain each document to you and who will then have both husband and wife sign each document. Since you will be required to make certain payments right at the closing, you must have your checkbook with you. You have $4,000 left in cash. Subtract that $4,000 in cash from the $18,000 purchase price. The remainder—$14,000—is the amount of mortgage you'll need. Your $4,000 is the down payment or equity.

Let's stick with the example we just cited: a $14,000 mortgage on an $18,000 house. Surprisingly enough, you can control to some degree—depending on your age and the house you are buying—the amount you'll have to pay on your mortgage each month. It works this way: The longer the mortgage runs, the smaller the monthly payments, or, the other way around, the shorter the time the mortgage is in effect, the larger the monthly payments.

Here are some actual examples. (See page 62 for figuring the interest alone.) For each $1,000 of mortgage money you'll borrow at 8 per cent, the monthly payments of interest and principal will total:

$9.56 on a 15-year mortgage
8.37 on a 20-year mortgage
7.72 on a 25-year mortgage
7.34 on a 30-year mortgage

Thus, if you succeed in getting an 8 per cent mortgage for 25 years, your $14,000 mortgage will cost you $7.72 a month per $1,000 or $108.08 a month. To that total you'll add 1/12th of your annual taxes and 1/12th of your annual insurance premium. The answer you get—once you've added taxes and insurance—is your *total* monthly mortgage payment.

Can you afford the monthly payments? The answer to this question will give you a double check on your ability to handle the mortgage. Your mortgage payment (including taxes and insurance) should equal, roughly, one week's take-home pay—but no more than that. If that mortgage payment is less than a week's take-home pay, you're in good shape. If it's more, then your expenses are out of line. Possibly you can lower that monthly payment by extending the term of the mortgage. Let it run 25 years instead of 20, for example. Or, if you now have the mortgage already up to 25 years and your monthly payments are still out of line, you'll do well to cut back on your estimate of how much you can pay for a house. Cut back by $1,000 to start. Do the necessary arithmetic over again—computing down payment, etc.—and see where you stand.

Different kinds of mortgages

Conventional mortgages are loans between you and the lending institution, based entirely on your credit and on the security of the property. There are no Federal agencies involved. All of the risk is assumed by the lender, and in case you can't meet your monthly payments, the lender can recover the money owed by forcing the sale of the property. By law, banks are told just **57** how long their longest-term mortgage can run, and they are told the minimum down payment they can accept in relation to the price of the house. In other words, even if your brother owned a bank, he couldn't give you a 40-year mortgage with no down payment. Such a financial arrangement would be against the law.

FHA and VA mortgages are Federal Housing Administration-insured and Veterans Administration-guaranteed loans. Because the Federal Housing Administration mortgage is insured (at a cost of ½ of 1 per cent of the amount outstanding) you benefit—your down payment or equity may not be as big as it would have to be with a conventional mortgage. A Veterans Administration mortgage allows a qualified veteran to mortgage up to most of the purchase price, in some instances reducing the need for a sizeable down payment. (Some banks, however, do demand 10 per cent down.) And VA mortgages usually carry a lower interest rate than conventional mortgages.

Getting a mortgage

Start by doing your arithmetic for the purchase of a home in your bracket. Then go to your bank's mortgage department. They'll give you an application to fill out. This form will bring out the information needed to show the bank clearly the credit to which you're entitled. The arithmetic you've done in this chapter—plus the realistic budget you've set up according to directions in Chapter Three—will show the bank that you are treating your personal finances in a businesslike manner. And that's what a bank wants to know.

Once your credit has been assessed, the mortgage department of your bank will be better able to give you an estimate of the mortgage amount you can afford. Of course, the bank can't give you a final commitment until you've selected a house, signed an agreement of sale and filed a mortgage application and their appraisers have inspected the house for mortgage-loan purposes. If you're building a *new* house, the bank will **58** inspect the plans and specifications. Finally, the bank decides on your application after reviewing your credit report and the property inspection report.

Those, then, are the details in financing a home of your own.

Buying a car

Just as you shop for the best purchasing price on the car you want to buy, you should be sure you have the best financing arrangement with which to make the purchase. There are several ways you can compute credit costs. But most ways involve percentages and annual rates of interest. They are so complicated that many prospective auto buyers throw up their hands in resignation and take the first source of credit they find. The best and simplest way to approach auto financing is to figure out what the loan costs you in dollars.

Here's an example of credit costs in dollars. If you had the necessary cash, you could buy an auto costing $3,000 for $3,000. But if you must borrow $3,000 for your car, then you must pay for the credit. For example, if your monthly payments to the credit source total $4,000 over the life of the loan, then the total dollar cost of your auto loan comes to $1,000.

Here is how you can compute your dollar cost when buying a car. After you've selected your car and all the optional equipment you want, you will be told the car's full selling price. Then the dealer will subtract your down payment, your trade-in, or both, from the selling price. The remaining total is the amount you must borrow.

You will then select the number of months you want the loan to run. Let's say you pick 36 months—three years—to keep the payments as low as possible. Once you tell the dealer three years, he'll tell you how much per month you must pay.

At that point, you should multiply the amount of each monthly payment by the number of payments to be made—36 in this case. Then compare the amount you borrow and the amount you repay. The difference—which may include life- and disability-insurance coverage—will be your dollar cost.

The chart that follows has been designed to make your **59** shopping for dollar costs as easy and as accurate as possible. We've put an example in the chart just in case you need help in figuring the various amounts. There is also space in the chart for you to write down and compare dollar loan costs from several credit sources. (And see center section, Page 25w., for an additional worksheet to figure the dollar cost of such a loan.)

		example		figures	
1	Total cost of the new car, including all optional equipment and all taxes		$3,150		
2	Less your: Down payment Trade-in TOTAL	$200 800	1,000		
3	The amount you need to borrow to buy the car		2,150		
4	Insurance costs of loan		52.28		
5	TOTAL amount to be financed		2,202.58		
6	Your monthly payments	74.08			
7	The number of such monthly payments	36			
8	The TOTAL amount you must repay (#6 multiplied by #7)		2,666.88		
9	Your loan DOLLAR COST (subtract #5 from #8)		464.30		

No matter where you borrow, here are a few tips that will help you to cut your dollar credit costs still further:

Put down the biggest down payment you possibly can. Consider a one-third down payment as minimum. That way you **60** automatically lower the amount you have to borrow. And since you have to pay for the use of dollars, the fewer you borrow, the cheaper your financing. That way, also, your debt will never be greater than the value of your car—an important point when you decide to sell.

Don't stretch out the loan to the maximum length unless you have to. You pay interest as long as the loan is outstanding. The quicker you can pay off the loan, the lower your costs will be.

Don't ever borrow money for the down payment. If you must do that, you really can't afford the car.

Watch out for "balloon notes" offered by some loan sources. They're the type in which the regular monthly payments on principal don't add up to the amount borrowed but fall short by several hundred dollars. When the last monthly payment comes due on such a loan, you have to make a whopping big final payment to make up the difference. Let's say you've borrowed $3,000 for 36 months. Normally your payments run about $96 a month, including an average of about $83 for repayment of principal. But in the balloon loan you pay only $86 a month for 35 months, and suddenly in the 36th month, you have to pay the difference all at once—about $360. Such loans look appetizing at first glance because each monthly payment is so low. Now you know why.

We have given you an idea of how to obtain a mortgage and an automobile loan, but for personalized assistance, visit your bank for an individual estimate.

Why not pay in one lump sum?

Paying with cash—not credit—isn't always the wisest thing to do. Strange as it may seem, there are times when it's better to take a bank loan—even if you have the cash. Here's why:

It's difficult for any young family to salt away dollars into a savings account, simply because the competition for every dollar you earn is fierce. So, if you do have a sizeable savings account, the smartest thing you can do is keep that account intact. Here are the benefits you'll get by taking out a loan: 61

First, you'll be obliged—obviously—to repay the loan. Nobody will ever force you to repay your savings account.

Second, while you're repaying the loan, your money in the bank will be drawing interest for you.

Third, the interest you do pay on your loan can be charged off against your income taxes as a tax-deductible item.

So, you can see, the cost of the loan is minimized by the interest your savings continue to earn and by the tax deduction you get on your income taxes.

Figuring your total interest on a mortgage

The amount of interest that you pay on a mortgage depends on two factors: the interest rate and the length of the mortgage. Obviously, you will spend less in interest if your mortgage is taken over a shorter term. And you will save even more if you can get a mortgage at lower than average rates. (One possible way to get a good rate: put up a large down payment. Discuss the idea with your banker. He will tell you exactly what rates you can get.)

Consult the table below to determine how much interest you will pay over a given length of time for each $1000 that you borrow.

For example, assume you plan to finance a $20,000 mortgage over a 20-year period at 8 per cent. Find "20 years" in the mortgage periods at the extreme left of the table. Then run your finger straight across the chart at the 20-year level until you come to 8 per cent. The amount you will pay—$1,008.80 per $1,000 of mortgage—is listed there. A $20,000 mortgage will, therefore, cost 20 times $1,008.80 in interest—or $20,176.00 in interest.

As you can easily see, the shorter the term, the less interest you will be required to pay. To demonstrate this another way, compare the monthly payments—which, of course, include both principal and interest—on a $20,000 mortgage at 8 per cent
over a 20-year period to the monthly payments on the same

amount ($20,000) at the same rate (8 per cent) over a 30-year period. Payments on the 20-year mortgage will be $167.30, while on the 30-year mortgage they will be only $146.75. But don't be fooled. Next multiply these figures by the number of payments involved in each transaction—240 payments over the 20-year period, 360 payments over the 30-year period. Thus, you will determine the total amount of the mortgage, or the amount that must be paid. For the 20-year mortgage the total will be only $40,152.00, whereas the total amount to be paid for the 30-year mortgage will run considerably higher, at a figure of $52,830.00.

	(per $1,000 borrowed)				
	5¾%	6%	6¼%	6½%	7%
15 years	$495.80	$519.20	$544.40	$569.60	$618.20
20 years	$687.20	$720.80	$754.40	$790.40	$862.40
25 years	$890.00	$935.00	$980.00	$1,028.00	$1,121.00
30 years	$1,024.00	$1,160.00	$1,217.60	$1,278.80	$1,397.60

	(per $1,000 borrowed)				
	7½%	8%	8½%	9%	9½%
15 years	$670.40	$720.80	$773.00	$827.00	$881.00
20 years	$934.40	$1,008.80	$1,083.00	$1,160.00	$1,239.20
25 years	$1,217.00	$1,310.00	$1,418.00	$1,520.00	$1,622.00
30 years	$1,520.00	$1,642.40	$1,768.40	$1,898.00	$2,027.60

A
**workbook
to help you plan
and record every aspect
of your family's
financial affairs.**

SOURCES OF INCOME PER YEAR

sources	last year	this year	next year
Salary			
Interest from savings accounts			
Gifts of cash on Christmas, birthdays, other occasions			
Money from sale of house, car, other items			
Tax refunds— state and Federal			
Payments from insurance policies			
Payments from profit-sharing plans			
Interest from bonds			
Dividends from stocks			
Profits from sale of stocks, savings bonds			
Other items			
TOTAL			

2w.

ESTIMATED WORTH OF ALL YOUR VALUABLES

value of:	last year	this year	next year
House			
Automobile			
Insurance policies			
Furniture			
Stocks			
Bonds			
Jewelry			
Silver			
Cameras			
Power equipment (mower, saw, etc.)			
Other items			
TOTAL			

3w.

LIST OF EXPENSES PER YEAR: Basic and Customary

item	last year	this year	next year
Shelter			
Food			
Clothing			
Medical expenses			
Transportation (car or other)			
Insurance			
Taxes			
Savings			
Maintenance and improvement of home			
Education			
Vacation			
Entertainment			
Contributions			
Gifts			
Liquor and tobacco			
Other items			
TOTAL			

4w.

LIST OF EXPENSES PER YEAR: Luxuries

item	last year	this year	next year
Travel			
Furs and jewelry			
Second car			
Color television			
Other Items			
TOTAL			

5 w.

SIMPLE BUDGET PLAN		January
expenses per month	the forecast	the reality
Shelter		
Food		
Clothing		
Medical expenses		
Transportation		
Insurance		
Taxes		
Savings		
Entertainment		
Other items		
TOTAL		

SIMPLE BUDGET PLAN		February
expenses per month	the forecast	the reality
Shelter		
Food		
Clothing		
Medical expenses		
Transportation		
Insurance		
Taxes		
Savings		
Entertainment		
Other items		
TOTAL		

6w.

SIMPLE BUDGET PLAN		March
expenses per month	the forecast	the reality
Shelter		
Food		
Clothing		
Medical expenses		
Transportation		
Insurance		
Taxes		
Savings		
Entertainment		
Other items		
TOTAL		

SIMPLE BUDGET PLAN		April
expenses per month	the forecast	the reality
Shelter		
Food		
Clothing		
Medical expenses		
Transportation		
Insurance		
Taxes		
Savings		
Entertainment		
Other items		
TOTAL		

SIMPLE BUDGET PLAN		May
expenses per month	the forecast	the reality
Shelter		
Food		
Clothing		
Medical expenses		
Transportation		
Insurance		
Taxes		
Savings		
Entertainment		
Other items		
TOTAL		

SIMPLE BUDGET PLAN		June
expenses per month	the forecast	the reality
Shelter		
Food		
Clothing		
Medical expenses		
Transportation		
Insurance		
Taxes		
Savings		
Entertainment		
Other items		
TOTAL		

8w.

SIMPLE BUDGET PLAN		July
expenses per month	the forecast	the reality
Shelter		
Food		
Clothing		
Medical expenses		
Transportation		
Insurance		
Taxes		
Savings		
Entertainment		
Other items		
TOTAL		

SIMPLE BUDGET PLAN		August
expenses per month	the forecast	the reality
Shelter		
Food		
Clothing		
Medical expenses		
Transportation		
Insurance		
Taxes		
Savings		
Entertainment		
Other items		
TOTAL		

9w.

SIMPLE BUDGET PLAN		September
expenses per month	the forecast	the reality
Shelter		
Food		
Clothing		
Medical expenses		
Transportation		
Insurance		
Taxes		
Savings		
Entertainment		
Other items		
TOTAL		

SIMPLE BUDGET PLAN		October
expenses per month	the forecast	the reality
Shelter		
Food		
Clothing		
Medical expenses		
Transportation		
Insurance		
Taxes		
Savings		
Entertainment		
Other items		
TOTAL		

10w.

SIMPLE BUDGET PLAN		November
expenses per month	the forecast	the reality
Shelter		
Food		
Clothing		
Medical expenses		
Transportation		
Insurance		
Taxes		
Savings		
Entertainment		
Other items		
TOTAL		

SIMPLE BUDGET PLAN		December
expenses per month	the forecast	the reality
Shelter		
Food		
Clothing		
Medical expenses		
Transportation		
Insurance		
Taxes		
Savings		
Entertainment		
Other items		
TOTAL		

11w.

A RECORD OF MONTHLY PAYMENTS	January
Rent or mortgage	
Auto loan	
Department-store charge accounts	
Personal loan	
Telephone	
Electricity	
Heating	
Other items	
TOTAL	

A RECORD OF MONTHLY PAYMENTS	February
Rent or mortgage	
Auto loan	
Department-store charge accounts	
Personal loan	
Telephone	
Electricity	
Heating	
Other items	
TOTAL	

12w.

A RECORD OF MONTHLY PAYMENTS	March
Rent or mortgage	
Auto loan	
Department-store charge accounts	
Personal loan	
Telephone	
Electricity	
Heating	
Other items	
TOTAL	

A RECORD OF MONTHLY PAYMENTS	April
Rent or mortgage	
Auto loan	
Department-store charge accounts	
Personal loan	
Telephone	
Electricity	
Heating	
Other items	
TOTAL	

13w.

A RECORD OF MONTHLY PAYMENTS	May
Rent or mortgage	
Auto loan	
Department-store charge accounts	
Personal loan	
Telephone	
Electricity	
Heating	
Other items	
TOTAL	

A RECORD OF MONTHLY PAYMENTS	June
Rent or mortgage	
Auto loan	
Department-store charge accounts	
Personal loan	
Telephone	
Electricity	
Heating	
Other items	
TOTAL	

14w.

A RECORD OF MONTHLY PAYMENTS	July
Rent or mortgage	
Auto loan	
Department-store charge accounts	
Personal loan	
Telephone	
Electricity	
Heating	
Other items	
TOTAL	

A RECORD OF MONTHLY PAYMENTS	August
Rent or mortgage	
Auto loan	
Department-store charge accounts	
Personal loan	
Telephone	
Electricity	
Heating	
Other items	
TOTAL	

15w.

A RECORD OF MONTHLY PAYMENTS	September
Rent or mortgage	
Auto loan	
Department-store charge accounts	
Personal loan	
Telephone	
Electricity	
Heating	
Other items	
TOTAL	

A RECORD OF MONTHLY PAYMENTS	October
Rent or mortgage	
Auto loan	
Department-store charge accounts	
Personal loan	
Telephone	
Electricity	
Heating	
Other items	
TOTAL	

16w.

A RECORD OF MONTHLY PAYMENTS	November
Rent or mortgage	
Auto loan	
Department-store charge accounts	
Personal loan	
Telephone	
Electricity	
Heating	
Other items	
TOTAL	

A RECORD OF MONTHLY PAYMENTS	December
Rent or mortgage	
Auto loan	
Department-store charge accounts	
Personal loan	
Telephone	
Electricity	
Heating	
Other items	
TOTAL	

17w.

RECORD OF AMOUNTS CHARGED

At space marked "account," write in the name of your account, whether it is grocer, department store, garage or drug store. Then write in the amount you have budgeted for this account for each month. Now keep a record of every charge and the date this charge was made. As the month progresses, you can see how much money you have left in terms of your budget. At the end of the month total your charges. If you are under the budget for several months in a row, you have allowed too much money for this account and should reduce the monthly figure in your budget. If you are constantly over the amount budgeted, you are either spending too much money on this item or have not allowed enough money for it in your monthly budget.

RECORD OF AMOUNTS CHARGED			January
account	amount budgeted per month	charges	date
TOTAL			

RECORD OF AMOUNTS CHARGED			February
account	amount budgeted per month	charges	date
TOTAL			

19w.

RECORD OF AMOUNTS CHARGED   March

account	amount budgeted per month	charges	date
TOTAL			

RECORD OF AMOUNTS CHARGED   April

account	amount budgeted per month	charges	date
TOTAL			

20w.

RECORD OF AMOUNTS CHARGED			May
account	amount budgeted per month	charges	date
TOTAL			

RECORD OF AMOUNTS CHARGED			June
account	amount budgeted per month	charges	date
TOTAL			

21w.

RECORD OF AMOUNTS CHARGED			July
account	amount budgeted per month	charges	date
TOTAL			

RECORD OF AMOUNTS CHARGED			August
account	amount budgeted per month	charges	date
TOTAL			

22w.

RECORD OF AMOUNTS CHARGED — September

account	amount budgeted per month	charges	date
TOTAL			

RECORD OF AMOUNTS CHARGED — October

account	amount budgeted per month	charges	date
TOTAL			

23w.

RECORD OF AMOUNTS CHARGED			November
account	amount budgeted per month	charges	date
TOTAL			

RECORD OF AMOUNTS CHARGED			December
account	amount budgeted per month	charges	date
TOTAL			

HOW TO FIGURE DOLLAR COSTS OF AN AUTO LOAN

1 Total cost of car, including all optional equipment and all taxes	
2 Less your: Down payment .... Trade-in .... TOTAL	
3 Amount you need to borrow to buy the car (subtract #2 from #1)	
4 Insurance costs for length of loan	
5 Total amount to be financed (add #3 and #4)	
6 Your monthly payments	
7 Number of such payments	
8 TOTAL amount you must repay (multiply #6 by #7)	
9 Your dollar cost (subtract #5 from #8)	

BALANCING YOUR CHECKBOOK

1 Your checkbook balance	
2 Subtract service charges as they are stated on bank statement	
3 Your new checkbook balance	
4 Bank statement balance	
5 Subtract the value of all checks written but not as yet paid by your bank	
6 New bank statement balance	
7 Add those deposits you have made which have not been recorded in current bank statement	
8 Which will give you a REVISED BANK STATEMENT BALANCE	

BALANCING YOUR CHECKBOOK

1 Your checkbook balance	
2 Subtract service charges as they are stated on bank statement	
3 Your new checkbook balance	
4 Bank statement balance	
5 Subtract the value of all checks written but not as yet paid by your bank	
6 New bank statement balance	
7 Add those deposits you have made which have not been recorded in current bank statements	
8 Which will give you a REVISED BANK STATEMENT BALANCE	

If all your deposits have been recorded, item #6 should coincide with item #3. If you have made deposits which have not been recorded, item #8 should agree with item #3.

26w.

RECORD OF BANK ACCOUNTS

name of bank	balance first quarter	balance second quarter	balance third quarter	balance fourth quarter
Savings:				
Checking:				
Other:				

27w.

RECORD OF STOCK HOLDINGS

stock	no. of shares	bought at price date	sold at price date	profit or loss

LOCATION OF IMPORTANT PAPERS

item	location
Will	
Deeds to property	
Insurance policies	
Stocks	
Bonds	
Other items	

29w.

CONTENTS OF SAFE-DEPOSIT BOX

30w.

RECORD OF INSURANCE POLICIES

	type of insurance and amount	what or who insured	beneficiary — if any	insurance company	policy number	insurance agent
1						
2						
3						
4						
5						
6						
7						
8						
9						
10						

31w.

CHAPTER SIX

Putting Your Extra Money to Work

Now—after clear thinking and planning—you find you have money left over, even after establishing the proper savings program and seeing that you have adequate insurance. What a happy and satisfying situation! But it's not time to sit back yet—not until you put that surplus money to work for you.

The wisest way to handle "leftover" money is to invest it in securities or other property that will not only yield a foreseeable return, but may also increase in value. Investing is one way of keeping your money protected against inflation, and it's also a way to build a nest egg for your retirement years.

Two worlds of investment

The two main areas to consider in the investment world are real estate and the stock market. Some hobbyists or specialists in certain fields may feel tempted to invest extra money extensively in stamps, coins, antiques or paintings, in hopes of an ultimate windfall. But aside from the accompanying fun of such an investment, the money-making results of this kind generally come only to the experts.

The theoretical approach to putting your money into real **97** estate and to investing in the stock market is the same. In real estate investing, for instance, you buy a building and then rent it out to gain current income. By improving this property you can increase your rents, or you can later sell at a better price than you paid, pocketing the profit.

In the stock market, you buy shares of a company's stock. If you sell the stock when its price is higher than when you purchased it, you make a profit. If you hold your stock and the company prospers and pays dividends, you have this added income.

That's the theory. But in practice there is the element of risk to consider. It's conceivable that the building you buy will need extensive repairs. Perhaps you will lose some of your tenants as their leases expire. You may end up with a loss instead of a gain. You must be able to carry your real estate through a couple of bad years, if necessary. And that common stock you bought can as easily take a nose dive.

Of these two investment worlds, the stock market is by far the more popular, for several good reasons. You can sell most common stock immediately, whereas you can hardly hope to unload a building, a home or an apartment house in one day. You can also sell your investment from wherever you happen to be, while you might have to show up at the site of your building to close the sale. And you might have to beat the bushes for a prospective customer for your building, whereas you don't have to look for buyers for your stocks. The buyers are at the stock exchanges and in the over-the-counter, or unlisted, market.

The stock market has one more benefit over real-estate investing, and perhaps this one is more to the point. You can invest small amounts of money in the stock market, but it takes several thousand dollars to swing a real-estate deal.

So perhaps your best bet—at least until you get your feet wet—is to start off slowly in the stock market. You might elect to invest through the ever-popular "Monthly Investment Plan" (MIP), or in one of the several mutual funds companies.

(See Page 102 for definition.) Or perhaps you'll choose to go it alone in the stock market, following the advice of a conservative stockbroker or the guidance of your bank. In the last analysis the decision is always your own.

How does the stock market work?

Regardless of your approach to investing in the stock market, you must first know what makes the market tick.

Investors put their money in what are called publicly owned companies—that is, companies owned by shareholders or stockholders. They invest in such companies for one reason only: to make money.

While there are varied ways to invest in the stock market, investors for the most part put their money in the common stocks of companies. When an investor buys a share of common stock, he becomes one of the owners of that company. As an owner, the investor shares in the future of the company. He stands to make money; he also stands to lose it.

There are three forces that will push up a stock's price. Let's take the fictitious Rien Corporation as an example.

The Rien Corporation's profits have been increasing for at least the past three years. This excites investor interest, pushing up the stock's price—even when the general economy is in a slump. Anything that spells more profits for Rien will attract investors. Some examples of profit-making news: Rien Corporation gets a multimillion-dollar contract from the Federal government, Rien Corporation successfully introduces a new product, Rien enters a new and profitable field via the acquisition of another company at a good price.

Assume that business is good and the broad economic outlook is bright. Investors then reason this way: Rien Corporation's business is bound to be good in such a climate. General prosperity spells increased profits for Rien!

Investors believe Rien Corporation is a sound investment. The fact that the investors may be totally incorrect in their assessment doesn't mean a thing. If investors clamor to buy **99** shares of Rien Corporation stock, then Rien's stock will rise in price.

Those forces that pull a stock's price down are the exact opposites of those that push a price up. If Rien is losing money —or is "slowing down" on profits—investor interest is likely to dampen.

The fact that business is in a recession, for example, will cause many investors to become cautious, to sell stock and to put their money in the bank until the prospects brighten. Such pessimism, even if Rien Corporation is doing well, may lower its value.

The fact that it's rumored Rien Corporation is a bad investment will discourage investors, despite the fact that Rien may actually be a sound investment. This reason stands out as the most difficult for newcomers to understand. "Why did the price of my stock go down?" such beginners ask. "It's a great, solid company." The only answer, many times, is the cryptic remark: "Nobody else thought so!"

Investors on Wall Street usually put their money to work with a specific objective in mind, or perhaps their aim is some combination of the three main investment goals: growth, safety and income. Here are the details you must know about each of the three types of investment:

Growth. These investors are willing to take risks in the market in the hope that they'll make big profits. Generally, such investors are young—under 45, say—and can afford a financial setback. They tend to concentrate their investments in the common stocks of aggressive companies whose potential for growth (that is, bigger and bigger profits) is excellent. When the market drops, growth investments tend to drop sharply. When the market is on the rise, growth investments often zoom up in price.

Safety. These investors aren't looking to get rich quick. Safety oriented investors simply want their investments to keep pace with rising inflation. For example, if inflation will so eat away

at a $100 bill in the next ten years that it will be necessary in

1976 to have $130 to buy what $100 will buy today, then the safety-oriented investor wants a conservative investment that will make his $100 build up to $130 or so by 1976. He asks no more than that. Safety-oriented investors buy conservative common stocks (the giant "blue chips"). These fall less in a declining market, go up more slowly in an advancing market.

Income. These investors attach primary importance to regular income, and sometimes put their money into high-yielding—and somewhat lower-quality—common stock in order to get maximum income. There are, however, many stocks of high quality that pay regular dividends year after year. It is important for such investors to remember that a stock that costs $30 a share and pays a dividend of $1.30 is a much higher-yielding stock than one that pays $2 a share but costs $100. Income investors must base their return upon the dividend as a percentage of the current market value of the investment.

Now that you understand the basic workings of the stock market, you may be tempted to draw out your savings and take a plunge in the market on your own. Don't do it!

No newcomer to the stock market should ever attempt to invest without the help of a broker, a banker or an investment counselor. Consider the case of Emily Long, 37 years old, recently widowed, and forced to raise four children on the proceeds of a $15,000 life-insurance policy and part-time employment. One day, while at her office, a business associate talked her into buying a stock that would "double her investment in no time." Emily needed money badly. So Emily took the gamble. She invested $8,000 in a $2 stock traded over the counter. Instead of going up in price, the stock fell to $1 a share. Emily's 4,000 shares, for which she had paid $8,000, were suddenly worth $4,000. She sold the stock and was $4,000 poorer.

Going it alone

If you invest on your own, you'll sign up with a brokerage house and become one of their customers. There are brokerage **101** houses all over the United States, not only in the big cities. Once you've proven to their satisfaction that you're a reputable individual, you'll be able to buy and sell all the stocks and bonds that you feel you can afford. Once you tell your broker where you feel your main investment interest lies, he'll gladly make buying and selling recommendations. And you'll do well to rely on his advice. One more suggestion: Don't expect miracles two days after you've bought your first round of common stock.

Mutual funds

If you buy a mutual fund, you'll be buying (along with thousands of other investors) a share of a multimillion-dollar collection of stocks and bonds—called a "portfolio" by Wall Streeters. Each mutual-fund share is worth exactly the same as each other share. And, taken together, all the shares are usually worth what the total stocks and bonds owned by the fund are worth on any one day. So, as the value of the securities in the fund's portfolio goes up, the value of your mutual-fund share rises. As the stocks and bonds decrease in value, so does the value of your share.

Mutual funds are an excellent means of investment for the man or woman with a relatively limited income and with little experience in the market. Professionals—men whose training and experience qualify them—decide which stocks and bonds the fund is to buy and sell.

Monthly Investment Plans

If you invest through the Monthly Investment Plan as your introduction to stock ownership, no matter how low your current income you'll find it a relatively painless process. MIP is a way for you to invest with as little as $40 every three months (or as much as you wish up to $1,000 a month) in any stock listed on the New York Stock Exchange. As an MIP investor, you are under no obligation to continue the plan. You can terminate it whenever you please.

102   The beauty of MIP is that it allows you to buy a portion of a share at a time, if that's all you can afford. For example, let's say you're interested in Rien Corporation's common stock, which sells for $80 a share. If you begin a $40-a-quarter investment in Rien Corporation, you'll own two shares of that stock after one year—assuming there are no wide swings in the price of the stock. Granted, two shares of an $80 stock is small potatoes, but it's not to be scoffed at. Starting to invest is more important than the size of your investment.

Using your bank when investing

After your money has begun to make money, and you need advice, counseling and management assistance in the overall handling of your increasing investments, you will discover that most banks have an investment-management service.

Some banks have highly developed systems of investment management, controlled by experts in the field and available to you when you open an investment-management account. Many banks also maintain funds in which investors with somewhat limited funds can put their money, just as they would invest in the mutual funds we've described.

When you have an investment-management account, your securities are deposited with the bank. The bank's investment-management department collects the income, and either deposits it in your account or disburses it in any way you wish. The bank buys or sells for you as you order it to do, and keeps full and accurate records of all such transactions. At stated intervals, the bank will report to you on the condition of your portfolio of securities and will supply you with all the information you need to keep your tax records straight. (Investment-management accounts will be accepted by some banks only in fairly sizeable amounts—this varies from bank to bank.)

The most important thing is the plus you gain from such an account—the advice of a number of experts whose business it is to know the market, know the trends, guide you in wise investing. Their help is not infallible, but it's perhaps the nearest you can come to prudent investment counsel.   **103**

How to read a stock table

If you live in a city, your daily newspaper is likely to have a stock table of financial transactions on the major markets: the New York Stock Exchange and the American Stock Exchange. If you are interested in investing in the stock market, the first thing you must learn is how to read the stock-market tables. The chore is not as complicated as it may appear.

Most full stock-market tables read like this:

	1		2	3	4	5		6	7
stock	(year) high	low	div. in $	sls. 100s	first	high	low	last	net change
Blue Chip Co.	36	21⅝	.60	2	34	34	33¾	33¾	−½

These figures mean that:

1 *Blue Chip Company stock thus far, this fiscal year, has had a range of $36 a share at its highest point, and $21.625 a share at its lowest point.*

2 *Blue Chip Company pays $.60 a year per share in dividends.*

3 *On the day covered by this table there were sales of 200 shares of Blue Chip's stock.*

4 *The opening-of-sale Blue Chip on this day was $34 per share.*

5 *At some time during this particular day, Blue Chip sold for as much as $34 per share, and as low as $33.75 a share.*

6 *The last sale of Blue Chip on this day was $33.75 per share.*

7 *The difference between the last transaction on this day, and the last transaction the day before, was a decline of $.50 a share—or ½ a point.*

Thus, if you owned Blue Chip common, the value of each share would have declined by $.50 during the 24-hour period covered from one closing to the next.

CHAPTER SEVEN

Choosing and Using Your Bank

If you needed a station wagon for your family—let's say four kids and one large dog—would you attempt to buy that wagon from a car dealer who specialized in small foreign cars, suitable for two very thin people and, possibly, their cat? Of course not. The idea is silly. You'd go straight to the dealer who meets your automobile needs—a man who sold station wagons.

We bring up the question simply to point out this fact: There are banks, and there are banks—and they are not all the same. Just as with auto dealers, you have to select and do business with the bank that has what *you* want in the way of services.

Easy? Yes, it is. But not to someone unfamiliar with the world of banking. For them, the subject is not quite so simple.

So let's spend some time talking about banks. Matter of fact, we'll even visit one together. When we've finished the visit, you will be able to pick your own bank with confidence.

Touring a bank

To begin with, there are three different kinds of financial institutions: savings and loan associations, mutual savings banks and commercial banks. **105**

Savings and loan associations. Usually called S and L's, they are organizations frequently owned by their members, and chartered to provide loans for professional builders, to grant mortgages to home buyers and to encourage thrift through programs of systematic savings, payroll savings, United States Savings Bonds and savings clubs. These associations are a fine old American institution, first established in 1831. In many communities they are just as important as the mutual savings banks.

Mutual savings banks. First started in 1816 in Philadelphia and Boston, these are nonprofit institutions, which specialize in savings accounts, savings clubs, and in granting mortgages. In some states they may also sell life insurance. Most mutual savings banks also sell money orders, United States Savings Bonds and traveler's checks. This kind of bank exists only in 18 states, primarily in the East.

Commercial banks. You will see as you read this book that commercial banks are often called the department stores of banking, because each one offers dozens and dozens of services. In general, every commercial bank in the United States—and there are over 13,000 located in the 50 states—offers at least these basic services: checking accounts, savings accounts, personal loans and mortgages. In practice, most commercial banks offer far more services than the basic ones we've mentioned. Consequently, the major differences between one commercial bank and the next hinge on the number of services offered.

You can see, then, that you must pick a commercial bank that offers exactly what you want. Otherwise, you won't be happy. You can also see, now, that neither an S and L nor a mutual savings ·bank can offer you all the services you must have month in and month out.

The best way to become acquainted with a commercial bank is to visit one. So that we can introduce you properly, we'll assume that you are a husband and wife taking the banking tour. Let's simply call you the Readers—Wes and Mabel Reader. And let's call our fictitious bank the Hometown Bank; a bank near you will offer some or all of these services.

Wes and Mabel Reader at the Hometown Bank

The guard approaching us is a retired policeman. He's here for protection, certainly. But his big job is to guide you to the right person in the bank—when you're in doubt. He'll also be glad to show you which deposit slip to fill out or tell you where to buy a savings bond.

The first point of inspection is the tellers' "cages"—the section of the bank that has probably changed the most in design over the years. Thirty years ago, tellers—they were almost all men in those days—stood locked in real cages. Today, there are no cages, and women are tellers as well as men. Tellers now stand out in the open with just the counter in front of them.

Perhaps Ed Abdel, one of the six tellers, can take a moment to tell us what he does here at the Hometown Bank.

"Be glad to, sir. The first thing, of course, is deposits. The Readers will make their deposits with me—both their savings and checking-accounts deposits. When they make their deposits, I must see that the deposit slip is filled out correctly and that the checks they've given me are made out properly on the front and correctly endorsed—signed on the back. And I must count the cash to see that its total agrees with the total written on the deposit slip. When the Readers make withdrawals, I make sure the check or savings withdrawal slip is filled out correctly. I count out the money withdrawn, being certain that I give them exactly the amount they've requested—in the denominations they prefer. And incidentally, if you should ever accidentally burn or tear any paper money, be sure and bring it to me. If more than half the bill is left, I can send it to the Federal Reserve for you. In most cases, they'll send you a check to replace the amount of the bill.

"I also make change, and I cash checks that are drawn on this bank—once I have the proper identification from the person presenting the check."

"What kind of identification do you ask for?"

"Usually a driver's license."

"Ed, you'll also take payments on a Hometown installment **107** loan when customers bring them in personally, won't you?"

"Yes. Some folks prefer to pay in person rather than mail in a check. I guess it's because they've come into the bank on other business and figure it's easier that way. Nice meeting you, Mr. and Mrs. Reader."

Some day you'll want to open a savings account and a checking account. You next meet the new accounts clerk, Miss O'Connor.

"Miss O'Connor, Mr. and Mrs. Reader are taking a tour of the bank. Can you spare a few minutes to tell them something about what's involved in opening both a savings and a checking account?"

"Certainly. Let's start with opening a savings account. First, you should determine whether you want to open an individual account—in other words, an account just in your name, Mr. Reader, or just in your name, Mrs. Reader—or a joint account. A joint account, of course, allows each of you to make deposits and withdrawals on the same account, without the permission of the other."

"Miss O'Connor, may we assume for our discussion that the Readers have chosen to open a joint account?"

"Yes. That will mean that withdrawals may be made by either Mr. or Mrs. Reader. When you open a savings account with this bank, you fill out a signature card just like this one in my hand. These cards are used to check your signature whenever you're withdrawing a large amount of money, taking valuables out of your safe-deposit box and on other special occasions. Some banks even have a television setup, so that your signature can be checked against a card at some central location when you're in a different department or even at a different branch of the same bank. The card will also request some slight personal information, such as address and date of birth, just enough to identify you, should the bank ever want to determine that you, Mr. Reader, are actually Mr. Reader. It's rare that you'll ever be asked, but we need that information—just in case."

"Miss O'Connor, how do the Readers identify themselves?"

"With their savings passbook or record—some banks have now eliminated passbooks and issue monthly statements, instead. That passbook or statement will contain a record of deposits, withdrawals, and interest paid by the bank to the Readers' account. That way, the Readers can tell how much money they have in their account. So much for the savings accounts.

"A checking account is one of the most useful services we offer here at Hometown Bank. Checks are really quite a convenience. They permit you to pay bills and make purchases in a safe, easy way—without the necessity of carrying around a considerable amount of cash. A checking account also provides an excellent means of keeping sound financial records. And did you know that checks can be used as legal receipts and proof of payment? Opening a checking account is just as easy as a savings account. Again, you will want to decide whether you prefer an individual account or a joint account."

"We would like a joint account, Miss O'Connor."

"Very well. Now one more question. Do you want a 'regular' checking account or a 'special' checking account?"

"We're not certain, Miss O'Connor. Would you describe them? Then we'll decide."

"A regular checking account calls for a minimum-dollar balance in the account. Just as long as that minimum is maintained each month, there is no cost for the normal number of checks written against the account. Nor do we charge for the number of deposits made to the account. But there is a regular monthly service fee. If the Readers' balance drops below the minimum-dollar amount, the bank then makes charges based on a published service-charge schedule.

"Now let me tell you about special checking accounts.

"Some banks call such accounts economy accounts or budget accounts. At Hometown, we simply call them special checking accounts. No minimum balance is required. And, believe me, that's a blessing to many young married people. There are two charges levied: a monthly maintenance fee, and a check charge **109** for every check drawn against the account. If a check is spoiled, by the way, there is no charge. This type of checking account is relatively inexpensive, and the owner of such an account has most of the benefits that go with a regular checking account: safety, convenience and a personal legal record of money paid out.

"While we're here, we ought to talk to the man you'll need to know if you decide to borrow money from Hometown, Frank Malley.

"Frank, this is Mr. and Mrs. Reader. We're showing them around the bank."

"How do you do. Won't you sit down for a minute?"

"Frank, we'd like you to review just what it is you do in this department."

"This is the place in the bank where we lend money. If you have a steady job and a credit history that shows you have repaid what you've borrowed, we'll be delighted to lend you money for any worthwhile purpose."

"Name some worthwhile purposes, will you, Frank?"

"Gladly. Want to buy a car? That's a good purpose. So's wanting to repair a roof on the house you own. So's wanting to pay medical bills. And what's more worthwhile than borrowing money to put a young person through college? There are literally dozens and dozens of good reasons for borrowing money. Others that come to mind are: to pay for a vacation, to consolidate several back bills, to build a recreation room in the basement, to buy a new refrigerator, a color TV set, perhaps a dishwasher.

"Mr. and Mrs. Reader, we could go on, of course. But we've made the point: You don't have to search far and wide to come up with a good reason for borrowing money."

"To continue, Frank, tell us why your department is called the installment loan department?"

"Because the money owed—along with the interest—is repaid to the bank in monthly payments, until the entire debt has been **110** wiped clean. Each such monthly payment is called an installment—a portion, as it were, of the entire debt. Thus, the name 'installment loans.' "

"Here's another question, Frank: How, exactly, do the Readers go about applying for a loan?"

"No problem. They come right to this department and ask to see any one of the three installment loan representatives. Let's say that Bert Higgins talks with the Readers. First thing Bert will want to know is what the loan is for. Then he'll give them an application to fill out. There are several types of installment loans: auto loans, personal loans on your signature alone, home improvement loans, tuition loans and appliance loans."

"Frank, why does a bank set up such loan categories?"

"There are different loan categories because each loan calls for a different contract between the Readers and the bank—and sometimes a different interest rate. For example, when the Readers take out an auto loan, they are, in effect, signing a lien instrument. Under such a contract, the bank retains a security interest in the car until the debt has been repaid. On an unsecured personal loan, on the other hand, the bank has no such collateral. The money lent on a 'signature only' personal loan is lent on the credit strength of the borrower. And when it comes to home-improvement loans, the money can sometimes be borrowed via FHA financing, which calls for a slightly lower interest rate."

"Thank you, sir. It's quite clear, then, why Bert first asks what the loan is for before giving us the loan application to fill out."

"Yes. And once that's out of the way, Bert can run down the questions on the application in no time. We want to know where you live, where you work—and for how long. We ask for references, your previous credit history, and where you bank. And we need to know how much a month you now pay in other installment loans. When we get that information, we evaluate it, based on our credit experience.

"Of course, we can't take any unwarranted risks. The fact is, the money we lend doesn't really belong to us. It belongs to **111** people like you who have deposited it here in savings accounts and through other means. If we were to lend money foolishly and lose it, all of us—banker and customers—would suffer. That's why we have to be so careful when we consider making a loan. Generally, we can make up our minds on the same day—sometimes in hours. And—you'd be surprised—most of the time we say yes."

"One final point. Will you explain collateral loans to the Readers?"

"Yes, of course. Collateral loans are made to any person who brings to the bank a valuable asset he is willing to lose if the loan is not repaid. Examples of collateral suitable for such loans are: stocks and bonds, ordinary life insurance without sufficient cash-surrender value, and savings passbooks. The interest charged on these loans is lower, because the bank takes much less risk."

"You mean, Frank, that the bank can always sell—cash in, so to speak—the asset, if and when the loan is not repaid, so the bank doesn't stand to lose the money it has lent?"

"Exactly. The rate on such loans is generally lower than on, say, signature-only loans."

"Thanks, Mr. Malley."

Within the next few years, you may be in the market for a house of your own. And when you start shopping for a house, you'd best start shopping for a mortgage at the same time. So let's go over to the mortgage department of Hometown and talk to Harry Morgan. We'll make our visit brief, because all of the mortgage information you'll need is given in Chapter Five of this book. However, it will be good for you to meet him today. That way you'll know where his department is located.

"Hello, Mr. Morgan. It's good to see you. These people are the Readers—Wes and Mabel. They wanted to meet you, even though they're not in the market for a mortgage right at the present time."

"Fine. Please sit down."

"In your experience, what do you suggest? Is it the best to buy a new home or an older one?"

"Folks such as you can often get a good bargain in an already existing house."

"At much of a saving, Mr. Morgan?"

"Yes, often. But there's nothing wrong with buying a house that's five years old. In some respects it can be better than a new one. For example, the shrubbery and the lawn are already in. Landscaping can be a very costly process, as you may know. I always try to get this point across to prospective house buyers: By buying an older house, they can sometimes save money on the purchase price and in equipping and maintaining the house, as well."

"Perhaps you can help the Readers if they decide to buy a home of their own."

"I certainly will. You know there's nothing more satisfying to a banker than having been instrumental in helping a family to home ownership. I enjoy every moment of it. Well, good day to you. And thank you for dropping by."

In Chapter Eight of this book, you'll find explained two of the many services performed by the trust department of a bank. Nevertheless, we ought to go upstairs to the trust department and meet its vice-president, Howard Bobb. There are five other trust department officers working with him.

As we go up in the elevator to the second floor, let us explain very quickly that only one-third of all the commercial banks in the United States have trust departments. And most of the time the word "trust" appears in the bank's name. Hometown is one of those exceptions. While Hometown offers trust services, the word trust does not appear in its title.

Mr. Bobb is waving us over.

"Good afternoon, Mr. Bobb. Meet Mr. and Mrs. Reader.

"Will you be good enough to explain to them—in general terms—just what a trust department's function is?"

"Gladly. Mr. and Mrs. Reader, we do many different things in the trust department. Some of the things we do may seem to **113** you to be quite removed from banking. Nonetheless, they are still financial functions—in a manner of speaking. We are authorized, for example, to act as guardians for children; we take care of money and property left by people who have died, and we manage the stocks and bonds of professional people—and others of means, of course—who don't have the time themselves.

"Let's take the case of an individual—a dentist, we'll say— who feels that his wife will need some guidance on handling the family finances. What is such a man to do when he's faced with the knowledge that upon his death his wealth may be dissipated, jeopardizing his children's well-being? Fortunately, he can come to us and arrange to put his money or his property in trust at the time of his death. In effect, that dentist is putting his money and his property—and sometimes the guardianship of his family—in the hands of someone he trusts."

"Mr. Bobb, isn't the trust function comparable to relying on an old friend to step in and take over, when we've passed on?"

"Broadly speaking, yes. But understand, please, that because a bank is a *corporate* entity it cannot die. Your friend, on the other hand, may die months or even weeks after you have died. Who, then, would carry on in his place? Furthermore, no matter how sincere your friend might be, it would be unusual for him to have the experience to handle the job as it ought to be conducted. Not only wealthy people, but families of average income come to us every day for help in managing their financial affairs, their children's financial future and other money matters. This is an area of banking more and more people are discovering and making use of. We like to think there's no situation or area that our trust department officers are not capable of handling."

Our final step on this tour is the basement, where we'll meet Will Clayton, who is the bank's supervisor of safe-deposit boxes.

Here's our elevator. When we step out of this elevator, you're going to have the feeling that you're in Fort Knox. Safe-deposit boxes are kept in a specially constructed vault, equipped with elaborate alarm systems. A vault attendant is on duty down there to identify everyone who comes into the area. He takes us to Mr. Clayton, who gives us a quick rundown on what goes on in his department.

He explains, "All of us have valuable papers and other assets to safeguard. The safest place for such things is a rented box in a bank's safe-deposit vault. We have over 3,000 boxes in this vault, and better than 85 per cent of them are rented right now. We rent those boxes by the year. The rental fee depends on the size of the box you choose. The smallest box, suitable for most people, rents for about 2 cents a day.

"When you rent a box, you'll be given two identical keys. At the same time, the bank will keep what it calls a guard key. Your keys and the guard key are different. Your safe-deposit box won't open unless your key and the guard key are used at the same time."

"What are some of the valuables people put in their safe-deposit boxes?"

"Actually, all kinds of things. Some items that come to mind are bonds, stock certificates, deeds, tax and other receipts, passports, birth certificates, military-discharge papers, citizenship papers, marriage licenses—along with the usual items of jewelry and heirlooms."

Now, let's go back up to the main banking floor, where we can sit down at a desk and review how to write a check, how to endorse a check and how to reconcile your bank statements with your checkbook balances.

Let's start with properly filling out a check. On Page 116, you'll see a typical check properly filled out. Follow the captions on that page for the right way to make out a check.

Then, on Page 117, see how to endorse a check properly.

Finally, let's go through the process of making your bank statement and your checkbook balance agree. To master that financial art, turn now to Page 119.

How to write a check

Below is a typical check. To make out a check, follow, one by one, the steps shown. Be sure to fill in all spaces.

1) The check number: If your checks are not already numbered, be sure to number them, as it is a great help in keeping records and balancing your checkbook. Write the check number on your check or record page, too.

2) The date: Contrary to popular opinion, a check may be dated on a Sunday or holiday, but do not write a future date on a check. Banks are not authorized to pay checks with future dates.

3) The payee: Be careful when drawing checks to "order," "cash" or "bearer." Such checks may be cashed by anyone. It is best that checks be made out to a specific person or company (the payee).

4) The amount: If the amount of the check as shown in figures differs from the amount as spelled out, the spelled-out amount is considered correct. To guard against alterations, put the figure right next to the dollar sign and start the written amount as close as possible to the left margin. Fill the unused space with a line.

5) The signature: The signature you use on your checks should correspond exactly with your signature on file at the bank. Never sign a blank check!

John Doe 100 Third Avenue, Anytown, U.S.A.	**(1)** No. *125* 1-2/210
(3) Pay to the order of *Telephone Co.*	**(2)** *6/14/67*
(4) *Sixteen* *75/100* —————— Dollars	**(4)** $ *16.75/100*

Anytown City Bank
1 Main Street, U.S.A.
0120   000   4   **(5)** *John Doe*

How to endorse checks

Before depositing a check which is drawn to your order, or before transferring it to another person, you must sign it on the back. This is called an endorsement. If your name is misspelled or incomplete on the face of the check, write your first endorsement in the same incorrect way; then, underneath it, sign your name correctly, using the signature you normally use on bank documents.

When you endorse a check without qualification, you assume the responsibility: *(1) that the check is genuine and valid, (2) that you have received value for it, and (3) that, if necessary, you will pay it yourself. (See qualified endorsement.) You may hold previous endorsers responsible for payment, just as any endorsers whose signatures succeed yours on the check may hold you responsible, if the bank upon which the check is drawn should refuse to honor it.*

Kinds of endorsements: *A blank endorsement—merely your signature—(see following page) transfers the ownership or title of the check to the person holding it at the time (the bearer). If the check is lost, the finder may cash it.*

A special endorsement names the person who must next endorse the check.

A qualified endorsement (without recourse) transfers title to a check, without making the endorser responsible for payment of the check.

A restrictive endorsement specifies what is to be done with the check and, for this reason, limits further endorsement and controls final payment.

Always remember that endorsing a check and depositing it in the bank does not mean you immediately have that cash to draw upon. The check must be sent to the bank which has the account against which the check was originally written. If that bank is in another town, it may take a few days for the money to be actually placed in your own account. Be sure to ask your teller how long each check takes to collect, so that you will be sure to know exactly when you may write checks against it. **117**

And one final warning: *Never borrow or lend a personal check. No matter how carefully you cross out the original titles and numbers on a preimprinted personal check, the machines that process the account will still read the original printing. This means that if you let someone else use your preimprinted check, the money may be drawn out of your account, no matter what your intentions. Always use your own checks, or a blank check, if necessary.*

Check endorsements illustrated

This check was drawn to the order of Ann L. Smith, whose name was misspelled as Anne L. Smith, and she passed it on in the following manner.

Blank endorsement to Joe Bink.	*Anne L Smith* *Ann L Smith*
Mr. Bink, then, transferred it with a special endorsement to Stella Golden.	PAY TO THE ORDER OF *Stella Golden* *Joe Bink*
Miss Golden transferred it with a qualified endorsement to Jonathan Bing.	*Pay to Jonathan Bing on order without recourse* *Stella Golden*
Mr. Bing signed a restrictive endorsement when depositing it to his account.	*For Deposit ONLY* *Jonathan Bing*

How to balance your checkbook with bank statement

Here is a simple system for balancing your checkbook against the statements you will receive from the bank each month. Of course, you will not be able to balance your checkbook or, for that matter, keep records of any kind, unless you are conscientious about making a note in the stub of your checkbook for every check you write. This notation is important because it provides the only sure method of knowing the amount of money you have spent, what you have spent it on, and how much money you have left in your account.

Different banks provide slightly different methods of keeping such records, but all checkbooks have some kind of stub or ledger for recording each check. Fill out the information when you write the check! Do not, under any circumstances, let it go until later in the day, or until the end of the week. Such carelessness will often throw even good money managers off the track, and soon their checks start bouncing. You will find the habit of recording your check when it is written of crucial importance in the maintenance of sound financial records.

To keep all your finances on a sound footing, keep your checkbook in balance. That way you will never write checks for money you don't have. The system to follow is an easy one. Simply deduct the total amount of money on the checks you have written, but which have not, as yet, been cashed, from the amount the bank has credited to your account. Then make any adjustments that are necessary—for example, deduct your service charges and add any recent deposits not shown on the bank's statement.

This is all you need to know to reconcile your checkbook balance with your bank statement:

1) When you get your statement from your bank, take out all the canceled checks and put them in numerical order (see #1 on Page 116) or by date, if your checks aren't numbered. Once you have arranged the checks, go through your checkbook stubs and put a mark on each stub for which you now have a canceled check.

119

2) Then, go back through your checkbook and write down on a sheet of paper the amounts of all the outstanding checks —those checks that have not yet been paid out of your account by the bank. Now, put down the amounts that you have deposited, but which the bank has not yet recorded on the statement. (Generally, such deposits are those that have been made after the bank statement was prepared.)

3) Finally, write down the service charges made against your account.

4) You are now ready to reconcile your checkbook with your bank statement. On the form below, write down in item #1, your checkbook balance. Then, in item #2, enter whatever service charges were made against your account. Subtract those charges from item #1. Item #3 will, then, represent your new checkbook balance. (Make a similar subtraction in your checkbook.)

5) At item #4, write in your bank-statement balance. Now, total up all outstanding checks and put that amount on the line at item #5. Subtract those outstanding checks from the bank-statement balance, and record the remainder at item #6 —your new bank balance.

6) At this point, if all of your deposits have been recorded, items #6 and #3 will agree, and your checkbook will balance.

7) If, however, you have deposits that do not appear on the statement, then at item #7, add those deposits to item #6. The answer appearing at item #8—your revised bank-statement balance—should, then, agree to the penny with item #3.

In instances where you cannot reconcile the balances, here are some places to check where you may have gone wrong:

1) Have you double-checked all addition and subtraction in your checkbook?

2) Have you carried forward any outstanding checks from your previous statement that are still outstanding? If you have any, they must be added to your outstanding-checks total.

3) Have you compared the amounts on your checks with the amounts listed on the stubs in your checkbook? You may have transposed totals in your checkbook.

4) Have you carried forward the correct balance from page to page in your checkbook?

5) Did you write a check and forget to enter it in your checkbook?

Once you've reviewed all the areas wherein you might have committed an error, if you still cannot find the mistake, bring your checkbook, together with your statement and your canceled checks, to your bank. One of the bank officers will be happy to help you—and unless there is something unusually wrong with your account, there is no charge for this service. Never delay. Go as soon as possible after you have received your statement—not a month later!

How to balance your checkbook

1	Your checkbook balance	$
2	Subtract service charges as they are stated on bank statement	$
3	Your new checkbook balance	$
4	Bank statement balance	$
5	Subtract the value of all checks written but not as yet paid by your bank	$
6	New bank-statement balance	$
7	Add those deposits you have made which have not been recorded in current bank statement	$
8	REVISED BANK STATEMENT BALANCE	$

(See center section, Page **26w.**, for more worksheets for balancing your checkbook.)

CHAPTER EIGHT

Look for These Extras from Your Bank

When you're picking a bank, keep in mind all the various services a bank can offer. You'll be surprised how much help a bank can be to you in many aspects of your life. Here are a few examples:

Certified checks

One bright day, Jim Montvale read a For Sale classified ad, stating that a sailboat "like new, paid $2,000" was being sold in a hurry for $1,000. The owner was moving in two days, the ad explained.

Jim called the telephone number in the ad, discussed the boat briefly and then drove out to see it. The owner, Bill Uscher, met Jim at the dock. Uscher explained he'd sold all his furnishings and now was very anxious to get rid of his boat. "I sure can't take it with me," he said.

"You're asking $1,000," Jim said, once he'd seen the sailboat and decided he wanted it. "But will you take $800 for it?"

"You're robbing me blind and you know it," Uscher said. "But the boat's yours—on one condition. I want cash, not a personal check."

"Impossible," said Jim. "I've got to have a check so I can show my insurance company how much the boat is worth. A bill of sale from you wouldn't be strong enough."

"Look," said Uscher. "Don't you understand? I'm not going to be here in another day. I never saw you before in my life. Who's to say your check won't bounce? I'm sorry. Cash or no deal."

Jim thought for a minute. "Will you take a certified check?"

"Of course," Uscher said, his face breaking into a broad grin. "Why didn't I think of that?"

The next morning, Jim withdrew $800 from his savings account, put it in his checking account and then had his bank certify his check by imprinting "Certified" across its face in a special ink. He drove out to Uscher's house and paid for the boat.

When the bank certified Jim's check that morning, the bank immediately withdrew $800 from his checking account. Under no circumstances, then, could Jim have taken all his money out of his account, making his $800 check worthless because of insufficient funds.

When a bank certifies a check, the bank guarantees to the person being paid that the money has been set aside to meet the check. A certified check is as good as cash—and safer! It's a special service only your bank can provide for you.

Automatic savings

Bob and Joyce Woodcliff lived the good life in their first two years of marriage. The upshot: They didn't save a dime. Fortunately, they weren't in debt, either. By their third wedding anniversary, the Woodcliffs still had no savings—but they now had a daughter. And when the fourth anniversary came, the Woodcliffs had no savings and two daughters.

In the four years that Bob had been married, he had received a $500 increase in salary. But, in that same time, his family's expenses had risen to match the increases in his income. No bills had accumulated, mind you, but no savings, either.

Fortunately, while the Woodcliffs were the kind of people who couldn't save, they did love each other. So, although they were concerned about having no money in the bank, they still weren't arguing and fighting about it.

But the big question in the fourth year of their marriage was this: Where would the money come from for a down payment on a home of their own? They just had to have a home soon. Two children and two adults in a small four-room apartment made for crowded living. The Woodcliffs knew they could borrow some money from Bob's family, but not enough for a down payment.

"If we didn't have it, we wouldn't spend it," Joyce said, one night late in January.

Bob listened and knew she was right. "If we didn't have it, we wouldn't spend it," he repeated.

On Valentine's Day, Bob gave Joyce a big kiss and a big heart-shaped box of candy. He then told her that this present would be the last little treat he'd be able to buy for quite some time. "We're going to take nearly a $1,000-a-year cut in salary," he told her. "Can we possibly swing it?"

"We'll have to," she said, trying not to seem depressed. "I've always said that if we didn't have the money, we wouldn't spend it. We'll get along." At supper she asked him: "Is business really that bad? Maybe you should look for a new job."

He nodded agreement and finished his supper.

For the next four months the Woodcliffs lived on a decreased income—$80 less each month than it had previously been. They didn't entertain. They didn't buy each other presents. They didn't go out on their usual Saturday night spree, a habit they'd had since they were first engaged. And, they didn't rack up any bills, either. They just spent less money.

In early July, Bob confessed. He called his wife into the living room and said: "Congratulations, honey. I knew you'd be a saver one of these days. And now you've come through with flying colors."

124   "What are you talking about?" she asked in bewilderment.

"You, my dear, have saved $400 since Valentine's Day!"

"That's nice," she laughed. "How?"

"I didn't have a cut in salary. On Valentine's Day, I went to our bank, filled out a form and had the bank automatically withdraw $80 a month from our checking account. That $80 went into a savings account I opened. We never got our hands on that money. So now we have $400, and by the end of the year we'll have $960. And by the end of next year we'll have the $2,000 we need for a down payment on the house."

That's one way to use another special service of your bank: the automatic-transfer savings plan. There are many other purposes in such forced savings. First, set up a savings goal. A sound incentive—one that makes your mouth water—is the best way to make yourself want to save. Here are some excellent savings goals: a vacation in Europe, college tuition for a son or daughter, the down payment on a house, an expensive hi-fi set, a sailboat, a remodeled kitchen.

Letters of credit

A month before Dr. Rolfe Oradell and his wife, Claire, set out on a month-long vacation in Europe last year, they decided this would be the opportune time for Claire to stock up for the antique shop she'd always wanted to own. They agreed that while in Europe, they would buy antiques for Claire's new business.

In planning the trip, they decided that they'd need, roughly, $3,000 to $5,000 to pay for the antiques. And then, of course, they would need about another $3,000 for their vacation expenses, including transportation.

"That's an awful lot of traveler's checks," Dr. Oradell told his banker, as he and Claire explained what they had in mind.

"It certainly is," his banker agreed. "But it's not really necessary to put it all in traveler's checks."

"You're not suggesting cash?" the doctor quickly asked.

"No. And I'm not talking about a batch of personal checks, either," the banker said.

125

What their banker was suggesting was that the Oradells should take some cash, which would be quickly converted into the local currency of each country they visited, a good supply of traveler's checks for their vacation costs (large denominations earmarked for hotel bills and car rentals, the remainder in smaller sums) and letters of credit for Claire's antique purchases. The letters of credit would be drawn on the bank's foreign-correspondent banks in the cities the Oradells would be visiting.

"That way," the banker explained to the doctor, "you'll have ready money to pay for the antiques, without having to carry cash or wads of traveler's checks to do it. Each of our correspondent banks—thanks to your letters of credit—will be authorized to give you up to $1,000 on each letter when you ask for it. And, to protect your letters of credit, we'll also give you a letter of identification."

"If I don't show the identification, the letter of credit doesn't work—is that it?" the doctor asked.

"Exactly," said the banker. "So keep your identification in a safe place away from—never *with*—your letters of credit. Now, have a good trip!"

"Thanks, I will," said the doctor.

His wife smiled. "And I'll bring you back an antique—just to show you how pleased I am," she said, shaking hands with the banker.

You can depend on letters of credit, too. As in the case of Dr. Oradell, you can use them abroad. Or—when the occasion arises—you can use a letter of credit while traveling on business or pleasure in the States.

Automatic bill-paying

Ida Westwood, 32 years old and a recent widow, managed her household finances rather well, considering the fact that she had four children. Ida had no big bills outstanding. She saved money regularly. And, thanks to the comfortable amount of life insurance that her husband had carried on her behalf, Ida

Westwood found herself able to invest money.

But Ida still had financial problems—a result of her poor memory. "I just don't have a head for dates," she would often tell her children.

Her difficulty with dates became serious one time when Ida forgot to pay not only the mortgage on her home, but an insurance policy on her life as well. Then, once she'd been reminded about her oversight (the bank holding the mortgage sent her a routine notice, and the insurance agent called her one evening to see what had happened) she promised to send the checks out immediately. Still, despite her good intentions, she forgot about them again.

By the time she'd finally paid both the mortgage and the life insurance policy, the next monthly payment on the mortgage was overdue as well. (She paid her life-insurance premiums annually.)

"What a bother it is to pay bills," she confided to a friend. And then she laughingly told the story of the forgotten mortgage and life-insurance bills. "I have the money," she ended her story. "But I just can't remember when to pay it out."

"You don't need a head for dates," her friend told her. "Let your bank handle the bookkeeping. Why, they'll even help you balance your checkbook when you have trouble with it."

Ida followed her friend's advice. And now Ida's financial life runs very smoothly. "My bank—not I—has the head for dates in my family," she now says.

Many banks can reduce your bill-paying chores, too. You simply authorize the bank to pay, for example, your monthly auto loan, the mortgage payments, or the premiums on your life-insurance policies. The bank automatically takes out of your checking account the money needed to pay these monthly bills.

Sending money by wire

Jim Borgen answered the phone in his home one Thursday evening not long ago. On the other end of the line was his son **127**

Jack, calling long distance from college.

"Dad," the boy said as soon as he heard his father's voice, "I need $75 by tomorrow. It's urgent."

His father said, "What's the matter?"

"Nothing's the matter, but if I have $75 before six o'clock tomorrow, I can buy all the books I need for the entire semester at secondhand prices. I'll save at least another $75."

"How am I going to get it to you? If you need it tomorrow, we can't count on the mail—not even airmail. I can go to the bank tomorrow morning and have the bank wire the money. If you call me around 10 tomorrow morning at the office, I can let you know where to pick it up. How does that sound?"

"Great, and thanks."

Aside from transferring money anywhere in the United States —the bank notifies by a special bank wire system its correspondent banks in other cities, ordering them to transfer funds to a specified person or company—banks can transfer funds from one community to another by bank money orders, personal money orders and bank drafts.

A bank draft is used for large sums and also for transferring money between countries. This enormous convenience makes it possible for you to wire money to someone in any foreign country through a bank, which will then convert your American dollars into local currency.

Many's the prodigal son or wandering student who has been rescued by the quick transfer of American dollars from home into pounds, francs, marks, or lire, through the magic of wiring money overseas.

Bank money orders and personal money orders may cost as little as 15 cents for any amount up to $250. These are ordinarily used when the money is to be spent locally.

Revolving loans

Ben and Mary Robbins noticed one autumn day, as they watched a football game, that their TV set was giving way fast.

128   "Darn," Mary said. "I can't put up with that annoying flicker very much longer. It disappears for a while, then comes back."

"You're right, honey," Ben agreed. "It really is getting to be a nuisance. Let's see if we can hold out until a cash sale."

Ben didn't have extra money on hand, but he knew he could get a good buy if he waited for this sale. So he decided to apply to his bank for a revolving loan account with personal-checking privileges. In this way he would have cash on hand whenever he needed it.

Mary and Ben went to the bank. They both knew he would have no trouble applying for such a loan. He had a good job record and his credit rating was O.K.

"Let's get enough money, so when furniture is on sale I can get a couple of comfortable chairs, too," Mary suggested.

Ben applied for a $480 revolving loan, and the Robbinses agreed to pay back any amount borrowed by regular, consecutive payments of up to $20 per month.

When Ben's application was approved, he received a booklet of blank checks. They were to be used against his revolving loan account whenever he wished. Ben put these checks away carefully in his desk drawer and waited through October and November for the television sale he had been anticipating. He used none of his credit during these two months, so no payments had to be made to the bank.

When December 1 rolled around, so did the awaited sale. Ben and Mary arrived at the store early to choose a set. They had cash in hand—or, rather, the special checks ready to draw against their revolving loan. Ben made out a check for $200, taking advantage of the big cash discount, and both Robbinses left the store well pleased with their carefully planned-for purchase. The bank would send a notice to let them know when the first payment would be due, and they could borrow up to $280 more, just by writing a check.

This is an example of sensible, well-justified borrowing. The money the Robbinses saved by paying cash at the right time more than made up for the interest charge on their revolving loan account.

The living trust

Dr. Edward Ungemach was a brilliant and busy surgeon—often called out of the city, even out of the country. Thanks to his professional ability he was, at 52, a wealthy man. Most of his money was invested in solid common stocks. Not for one minute, however, did Dr. Ungemach ever consider himself an investment expert. He looked upon himself solely as a surgeon who had the wisdom and foresight to invest early for his retirement years.

Years ago, Dr. Ungemach, with the help of his lawyer, set up a living trust administered by his bank. Consequently, the bank assumes his worry about buying and selling the stocks in his portfolio. His trust department invests his money, keeps his funds under constant scrutiny and invests the income that the portfolio earns.

The living trust frees Dr. Ungemach—and thousands of other busy professionals and executives—from the bother and worry of the innumerable details involved in the protection, supervision and custody of securities.

The living trust set up by Dr. Ungemach is revocable. This means he can cancel it whenever he wishes, or he may amend the trust as he sees fit.

And when the time comes for Dr. Ungemach to retire, he can spare himself the need to pull up his banking roots, should he move to another city. His bank's trust department can continue to provide the same trust services in his absence. In effect, his trust department is his financial alter ego.

If Dr. Ungemach wishes, he can use his living trust in other ways. He can include provisions for the protection of minor beneficiaries, if he has any. Or, he can have his lawyer design his living trust to administer his wishes for the distribution and management of his assets when he dies.

The trust department of a bank is also set up to provide an executor, should such be requested by a person drawing up a will. The trust officer who fulfills the executor role understands

130 how to settle an estate with diplomacy and efficiency.

These are but two of the many services performed daily by the officers of a bank's trust department. There are many more. Your bank's trust department will be glad to discuss your wishes in this area with your lawyer and with you, in confidence, and at your convenience.

Summary

The examples we've just covered in case histories represent only a small portion of the broad range of services a full-service commercial bank offers.

Briefly, a bank will also help you get a low-cost, long-term college-student loan, establish a Christmas club account, rent a safe-deposit box, buy United States Savings Bonds. It will also make personal loans and many types of business loans.

It is the business of your bank to provide any necessary personal and professional financial advice you may need. You'll find that—provided you've chosen your bank wisely—you will be able to call upon your bank for a wide range of invaluable services, plus the intangible assistance of personal help and advice. No matter what your problems are in managing and planning your life and your family's affairs, you can depend on a good full-service bank.

LOOK FOR THESE EXTRAS

SERVICES OFFERED BY MOST FULL-SERVICE COMMERCIAL BANKS:

checking accounts	savings accounts	special savings
Special	Individual	Retirement trust
Regular	Joint guardianship	Insurance
Business		Christmas club
		Vacation club
		Babies' security
		College funds
		Savings bonds
		Certificates of deposit

SERVICES OFFERED BY MOST FULL-SERVICE COMMERCIAL BANKS:

loans	management aids	other
Auto	Investment counseling and management	Certified checks
Home improvement	Trust services	Traveler's checks
Mortgages	Automatic bill-paying plans	Money orders
Personal	Stock-dividend deposit	Wiring money
Business		Safe-deposit boxes
Revolving		
Tuition		
Credit cards		

CHAPTER NINE

Bank Credit Cards

A charge card issued by a bank offers a new kind of shopping convenience. This type of card has become a money management tool enabling a qualified individual to buy products and services quickly and conveniently, on credit, without having to carry cash or half a dozen cards from separate stores or credit card services. And, perhaps best of all, this kind of card gives the holder one bill once a month instead of a dozen bills, from a dozen different sources, that arrive at many different times throughout the month.

There are several kinds of bank charge cards, varying from those issued by a single institution to those backed by a nationwide—in some instances worldwide—association of banks. The latter are usable almost any place, for almost any services or goods you can imagine. In addition, some of these cards offer other built-in conveniences: widespread check-cashing or cash advance privileges, for example, or what are known as "instant loans." In this chapter we'll explore the kinds of bank charge cards available, and the advantages they offer. We'll take a look at how this system of credit came into being and how it has spread and grown in the brief time since the first bank charge card was introduced.

Why a bank charge card?

"I thought you'd never get here," Alice Pratt told her husband as she helped him unload his luggage from the car.

"That's the shoe business, honey," Dick answered, picking up a bag and heading for the house. "I'll admit it's a bit unusual to stay five days longer on the road than I'd expected, but it's happened before and probably will again."

"How did you manage about money?" Alice asked. "You only planned on staying a week."

Dick held the door open for her. "Credit cards," he answered. "Look." He took out his wallet and fanned a collection of seven plastic cards for her to look at. "With these, I'm equipped for just about any emergency."

"So many? But I guess they're useful, all right," Alice agreed. She went into the kitchen and shortly supper was on the table. When Alice brought in the dessert she brought up the subject of credit cards again.

"Why do you need so many credit cards?" she asked.

"Because some places will accept only certain cards, and other places accept different ones. Some are only good in restaurants, for instance. One I have is accepted by a number of hotels, but not by all. One is for an airline. That's how it goes."

"Did you know," Alice asked him, "that our bank issues what they call charge cards that are accepted by a lot of merchants in town, including several department stores? I saw an ad about it the other day. Wouldn't it be smart for me to have such a card? We'd get only one bill a month, instead of such a bunch of them."

Dick looked thoughtful. "If I could use that same card when I travel, it might be wiser for me to have one bank charge card instead of that collection I now carry around in my wallet. Listen, Alice, I'll look into this business of bank charge cards first chance I get. A card for each of us, one bill each month, sounds to me like a great idea."

How it all began

The paper, metal or plastic card and plate that verifies a person's credit has been in use for considerable time. But it is only since World War II that this financial tool has become a major force in our economic system. And it is only in the past few years that the many different types of cards now available have proliferated.

"Charge account" cards and plates were first in general use. They were issued by merchants to their best customers—the affluent few who were the largest purchasers and the best credit risks.

As the economy expanded, so did the number of families that were good credit risks. Millions of people traveled more, bought more goods and services, became accustomed to having more money to spend and to managing the spending of it. This led to a new concept—a credit card that could be used for charging at various places, not just one.

Travel and entertainment cards

Cards for charging travel and entertainment expenses were the next of the new breed to appear. These provided their owners with credit at specified hotels, motels, restaurants, airlines and gift outlets. Cards of this type are usually held by the heads of families with incomes of $10,000 or more. To use this kind of card, a person must pay an annual membership fee—usually $12 to $15.

These plans do not usually charge interest for extended payments by the cardholder; the cost of carrying this credit is part of the reason for the annual membership fee. Holders who habitually do not pay their bills promptly are denied further use of their cards.

While various types of businesses honor these cards, they are not all-purpose. Generally their use is confined to businesses that deal with travel and entertainment. (Costs to the cardholder and to the merchant tend to be slightly higher than with genuinely all-purpose bank credit cards.)

Another card of this sort is issued by one company—such as a major oil company with service stations in a large area or **135** throughout the country. These cards can often also be used at some hotels and other establishments, but their chief purpose is to create customer loyalty for the company that issues them. Costs of all credit—risks, checking, paperwork and so on—are borne by the issuing company, and these costs can be substantial. They represent a major part of the company's cost of selling its products or services, and are therefore a factor in the company's prices to the customer as well. Some issuers of such cards use lists of their cardholders' names as mailing lists for the direct-mail selling of insurance, appliances and other items.

In this category, too, is the Air Travel Card, honored by airlines and many hotels as well. This card requires the cardholder to keep $425 on deposit with the airline that issues the card. Some businesses, not a part of the airlines credit system, will accept such a card as a proof of credit worthiness of the holder.

All these kinds of cards—including the one issued by an individual retailer or service establishment, the travel and entertainment and air—are still in use.

Some of these do not carry interest. When this is the case, the merchant must finance the cost of funds outstanding until bills are paid, assume all credit risks plus the cost of handling his accounts. These expenses must then be figured into the selling price of the merchandise. The cost of handling credit accounts in a large retail establishment is well over 8 per cent, as estimated by an impartial 1968 survey. Other forms of credit offered by merchants—revolving credit plans, for example—carry interest or carrying charges. In some cases these are intended to provide the merchant with additional profit.

The beginnings of bank charge plans

Bank charge card plans were started in the early 1950s, but the most famous system, in which various banks honor and exchange sales slips involving each other's charge cards, began to issue cards only a short time ago—in 1967. It was originally called the California Bankcard Association and later known as the Western States Bankcard Association. It was started by four of California's leading banks who agreed to issue the same charge card jointly.

Using the name "Master Charge," cooperation consists of exchanging sales slips submitted by any merchant signed up by one of the member banks and allowing cardholders to charge with any of these merchants. The banks set a credit limit for each cardholder, so that no person can charge beyond his ability to pay.

How bank charge cards work

Most bank charge cards have a number of things in common. They are issued by banks to credit-worthy people, who receive one monthly statement covering all purchases made by the cardholder during the month, regardless of merchant, location or type of merchandise or service. These cards are honored by stores, professional offices, other businesses and service organizations that have been enrolled by cooperating banks. These are easy to spot; they display the symbol of the particular bank charge card or cards they accept.

If the bank charge cardholder elects to pay his entire monthly bill within a period specified by the bank there is no cost for the service. Or he may choose to pay a specified minimum amount of his total balance for that month or an amount above the minimum. If he does, a service or interest charge is added to the unpaid balance.

One great advantage of bank charge cards is that they bring charge privileges within the reach of many to whom such cards were not previously available. The majority of bank credit cardholders have incomes of $7,000 or more per year. Income plus an established good-payment record plus stability—these are the criteria by which an applicant for a bank credit card is judged.

Interchange—what does it mean?

The present trend in bank credit cards is interchange, permitting a cardholder to use his card not only with merchants enrolled by his own bank but also with thousands of other merchants and services that agree to honor cooperating card plans. Regional interchange covers a section of the country; national interchange covers the entire country; international interchange blankets large parts of the world, tying regional systems' cards and individual banks' cards into a broad, cooperating network.

There are two such national and international systems. One is Interbank Card Association under which many regional systems and independent bank card plans operate. The second is Bank-Americard, owned by the Bank of America of San Francisco.

Interbank Card Association members' cards carry the small letter "i" in a circle in the lower right-hand corner of the face side of the card. In addition, most of the banks belonging to the Interbank system use the Master Charge name—a service mark whose graphic symbol is two interlocking circles, one red, one orange. Interbank is an association of bank members who operate charge card plans, formed to facilitate the national and international interchange of bank charge cards. The founding members include California Bankcard Association and Marine Midland Bank, among other successful pioneers in the bank charge card field. BankAmericards are designed in horizontal stripes of blue, white and yellow.

In early 1970 there were approximately 36,460,000 cardholders and 700,000 merchant outlets in the world enrolled in Interbank. At the same time, there were 29,500,000 Bank-Americard holders and 646,000 merchant outlets, while 78 of the 100 largest banks in the United States offered credit cards.

Besides these charge cards, some banks issue special service cards. Among these are check credit cards, which permit writing checks up to a certain amount without having that amount in cash on deposit—in effect, "instant loans"—and identification cards that vouch for the holder when he wishes to cash a check or establish credit.

Why bank cards?

Considering all the various kinds of credit and charge cards, bank cards have certain outstanding advantages. For example, from the merchants' point of view: the banks assume all credit risks, provided the merchant follows the specified procedures regarding limits of credit to be extended, checking with verification centers before extending credit and processing sales slips promptly in accordance with the procedures set up. Discounts charged to the merchants, because they are set by competition, are generally lower than the costs of other credit plans, and there is virtually no need for the merchant to have a credit department of his own. Interest need not be paid on loans to cover outstanding credit, because such loans are not necessary—the merchant's account is generally credited with the amounts of one day's sales by the following day.

The cardholder profits, too. No charge is made for issuance of the card. If payment is made within the period specified by the bank, there is no interest charged, no carrying charge. Extended payments are available, however, if this is what the customer prefers; in this case, a service charge is added to the unpaid balance. The cards are acceptable in many places. If they are a part of a national card system, the holder can use them in all of the United States; if part of an international system, in Europe, Mexico and Japan as well. And such cards are often acceptable to many establishments that will honor no other types of credit cards.

In addition, in most cases the holder can use his card when he needs cash—$50 or more. He need only present his card at any bank honoring it, and the bank will make an immediate loan available. This can be handy, because in spite of the many uses of credit cards, cash is still necessary in some cases!

With bank cards acceptable in so many places, for so many goods and services, this card cuts down on the number of credit cards a holder would otherwise carry—and on the number of monthly statements he receives, on the number of monthly checks he must write. If the card is lost or stolen, the holder need only notify his bank as soon as the loss is apparent to him, and he has no liability for purchases made by someone else using his card. Sales slips give the cardholder an accurate record of his **139** purchases—and are an aid to budgeting and to bookkeeping.

A special occasion

About two weeks after their conversation in the early part of this chapter, Dick Pratt came home one evening to tell his wife, "Got a present for you, Alice."

She smiled at him. "Why? It's not my birthday—what's the occasion?"

"The occasion is a total revision of our bookkeeping system," Dick told her. "Remember, I said I'd look into the business of bank credit cards? Well, I did—and does it ever make sense!" He fished in his pocket and brought out a card. "Here's yours, and I have mine—and I can get rid of most of the others that I carry."

"Is it good in many places?" Alice asked, taking the card and examining it.

"A lot more than we thought when we were talking about it the other night. This card is good not only all over town here, not only in the outlying area, but just about everywhere in the United States and in a lot of foreign countries besides. And, as you said when you first brought the matter up, we'll get just one bill at the end of each month, have just one check to write. More, if we want to charge some large item, we can pay for it over a number of months, just as if we bought it on the installment plan at the store, and the carrying charge will be no more—it may well be less. Not only that, but if we find ourselves suddenly pressed for cash, this card will get us an immediate loan at any bank honoring it—and that's a lot of banks! How do you like that?"

Alice nodded emphatically. "I like it," she said. "It's a great idea. Now get washed up—dinner will be on the table in five minutes."

Index

144